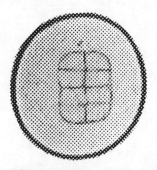

EARLY LIFE HISTORY OF MARINE FISH
The Egg Stage

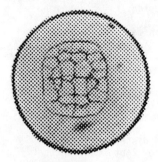

EARLY LIFE HISTORY OF MARINE FISH
The Egg Stage

Gotthilf Hempel

A Washington Sea Grant Publication
Distributed by University of Washington Press
Seattle and London

The series of lectures on which this publication is based were supported
by grant number 04-5-158-58 from the National Oceanic and Atmospheric
Administration to the Washington Sea Grant Program.

The U.S. Government is authorized to produce and distribute reprints
for governmental purposes notwithstanding any copyright notation that
may appear hereon.

Library of Congress Cataloging in Publication Data

Hempel, Gotthilf
    Early life history of marine fish

    Bibliography: p.
    1. Marine fishes--Development. 2. Fishes--Develop-
ment. 3. Fishes--Eggs. 4. Fishes--Fecundity.
I. Title.
QL639.25.H45   597'.03   79-14549
ISBN 0-295-95672-0

CONTENTS

ILLUSTRATIONS

TABLES

FOREWORD

The National Sea Grant College and Program Act of 1966 initiated a university-based effort to develop and preserve the nation's marine resources. One thrust of this program is to strengthen the education and training of students to meet the manpower needs associated with the management of marine resources. The ensuing financial support has enabled the College of Fisheries at the University of Washington to establish an open chair for guest lecturers.

Normally, in the budgetary processes of a university it is difficult to establish such a position and keep it open continuously. However, as a result of this Sea Grant support, the College of Fisheries has been able to invite some outstanding contemporary biologists from Canada, the United Kingdom, FAO Rome, Australia, and West Germany. There are immediate benefits accruing to students and faculty members both from the lectures and the close association with overseas visitors. A widespread benefit is the publication of the lectures in book form, and the present edition based on 1975 lectures represents the latest effort in this endeavor.

Professor Doctor Gotthilf Hempel was born in 1929 in Göttingen and received his schooling there and in Berlin, followed by university training in Mainz and Heidelberg during the post-war years. By 1952, he had earned his doctorate and launched immediately upon a decade in fisheries investigation from research stations in Wilhelmshaven, Helgoland, and Hamburg.

A three-year period followed with international assignment for UNESCO and FAO. In 1966 he was appointed professor of fisheries biology at the Institute of Marine Sciences, Kiel University, a post he still occupies. In addition to his regular teaching duties, Dr. Hempel has played an important and decisive role in international fisheries affairs and has served as a frequent chairman of symposia. He served from 1966 to 1976 as president of the International Association of Biological Oceanography.

The present publication appears some time after the lectures were delivered due to the author's wish to make a very exhaustive review of the literature on the early life history of fishes from the time of gonadal development to the appearance of a free-swimming larva. For the North American reader this book provides a unique entry to the rich European literature on this phase of the early life history of marine fish.

Ole A. Mathisen
July 1979

PREFACE

There is a growing interest in the study of the early life history of marine fish. The fact that fish eggs and larvae form part of the marine zooplankton ties them closely to the dynamics of this most important component of the marine ecosystem. The connections of the early life history stages to size and composition of the parent stock, and to subsequent recruitment, prompted fishery biologists to study the ichthyoplankton in order to monitor trends in single fish stocks and multispecies fish populations and to forecast recruitment for management purposes. However, in most cases they did not find clear correlations between eggs or larvae and parent stock size and subsequent recruitment. This called for laboratory and field studies of the variations and causes of high mortality in the early life history. Different survival strategies in species with millions of eggs versus those with several thousands are still the subject of speculation. For practical purposes, the lack of understanding of the early life history phase is still the major bottleneck of mariculture.

So far, no attempt has been made in literature to introduce students to the state of knowledge and concept in the study of the early life history of marine fish. This publication originated from a series of lectures given at the College of Fisheries, University of Washington, in March/April 1975. More recent literature has been incorporated in the text. This volume gives a brief general description of development and objectives of the study of the early life history of fish and continues with the development of the egg cells and with variations in fecundity and egg size in marine fish. The incubation period of demersal and pelagic eggs is considered mainly in relation to ecological aspects. A similar publication on the larval stage is planned.

The author is most grateful for the encouragement and patience of Professor Ole Mathisen from the planning of the lectures to the final preparation of the manuscript. He also acknowledges the assistance of Dr. I. Hempel and Dorothy Beall in editing the text. The lecture notes were used as supplemental text at the College of Fisheries in a lecture series, "The Early Life History of Marine Fishes," taught by Dr. B. S. Miller. He has corrected the manuscript and eliminated some ambiguities detected by students in his course. A final review was made by Dr. A. C. DeLacy who formerly taught this subject matter at the College of Fisheries. I express my thanks to these two colleagues for greatly improving upon the readability of this manuscript.

Gotthilf Hempel

INTRODUCTION

THE STUDY OF EARLY LIFE HISTORY OF FISH
AS PART OF MARINE FISHERIES BIOLOGY

W. F. Royce (1972) identified three areas of work related to fisheries in their broadest sense, which require the participation of scientists: 1) management of the fishing of public resources; 2) protection and enhancement of the environment; and 3) aquaculture. Problems of early life history of fish are related to all three fields:

1) *Fisheries management* must take into account the fact that a fish stock is a renewable resource only as long as the reproductive potential of the parent stock is kept on a sufficiently high level. The problem of recruitment has been discussed in detail by Cushing (1973). Furthermore, management depends largely on stock estimates and recruitment forecasts, some of which are based on egg and larva surveys.

2) *Protection and enchancement of the environment*. At first look it appears little can be done to improve survival of marine fish, compared to the possibilities, for example, in salmonids in freshwater. However, protection against marine pollution opens an entirely new field of research. Early life history stages are particularly sensitive to pollutants such as hydrocarbons and heavy metals. Not only pollution and eutrophication but the whole problem of coastal management comes into focus when studying the early life history of marine fish, many of which have their nurseries near the coast, where they are endangered by silting, gravel dredging, and land reclamation.

3) *Aquaculture*. True husbandry of fish depends on the full control of early stages. In commercial sea fish aquaculture, there are only very few examples in which the whole life cycle is kept in captivity and is fully controlled. There are, however, attempts, with

1

Fig. 1 G. O. Sars (1837-1927).   Fig. 2. V. Hensen (1835-1924).

increasing success, to proceed beyond the present common practice of
fattening wild-caught young sea fish.   An ultimate aim of modern
aquaculture is the selective breeding of marine finfish in the same
controlled way as with trout and carp.

Fisheries biology is one of the oldest branches of applied ecology.
Because of their economic importance, finfish such as salmon, carp,
cod, plaice, halibut, tuna, and herring are among the most investigated
organisms;   their life history and their relation to the environment
have been the subject of many studies, despite the fact that most
marine fishes are relatively difficult to keep and particularly
difficult to breed in captivity.   Thanks to the information gained from
statistics of commercial fisheries and from scientific sampling of the
fish stocks, concepts of population dynamics have been developed which
are more sophisticated than many approaches used in other branches of
ecology.   This, however, is not yet true for the study of the early
life history stages of fish.   The dynamics of the populations of fish
eggs and larvae, as well as their basic ecological requirements, are
very different from those of the adults; their study is a rather
independent branch of fisheries biology, which has moved into the phase
of mathematical modeling only very recently.

The life history of most teleosts can be divided into four phases:
egg, larva, juvenile, and adult.   The egg phase or incubation period
lasts from fertilization to hatching when the larva leaves the egg
shell.   The larval phase ends with metamorphosis, and the juvenile
phase with sexual maturity of the fish.   The first two phases are very
different from the later ones in most aspects of their biology.   There
are also considerable differences in the early life history between
marine and freshwater fish. The majority of marine fish eggs and larvae
are parts of the plankton;   they are frequently referred to as
"ichthyoplankton."   However, several marine fish, particularly in
shallow waters, lay demersal eggs or fix them on floating objects (a
few are viviparous), supressing more or less a free-living larval
phase.   In freshwater, fish eggs (and sometimes even larvae) stick
mostly to the substrate.   Brood care is more common in freshwater

Fig. 3.   E. Ehrenbaum (1861-1942).

Fig. 4.   J. Hjort (1869-1948).

fishes than in sea fishes.   In many respects the study of the early
life history of marine fishes is more related to plankton research than
to the usual approach and methods of fisheries biology.

In contrast to the adult (and often also the juvenile) phase, there is
little exploitation of larvae and fertilized eggs, except in East Asia
for some commercial fishery for fish larvae for human consumption, and
for collecting the larvae and juveniles of milk fish, mugilids, and
eels for stocking inland waters, lagoons, and aquaculture
establishments.   Furthermore, there is a market for the highly priced
unfertilized roe of sturgeon, lumpsucker, herring, and cod.

HISTORICAL NOTES ON THE MAIN LINES
OF ICHTHYOPLANKTON RESEARCH

Despite the lack of direct commercial interest in fish eggs and larvae
the study of the early life history of fish was an important element of
fisheries biology from its onset about 100 years ago.

When G. O. Sars (Fig. 1) was asked by Norwegian authorities to study
the biology of cod in order to understand the fluctuations in the
Norwegian cod fishery in the Lofoten area, he found and identified in
1865 the floating cod eggs near the surface and described the pelagic
egg stage as an important part of the life history of marine teleosts
(Rollefsen 1962).   At the same time the concept of oceanography as a
multidisciplinary science slowly emerged.   The importance of surface
currents for the transport of eggs and larvae was recognized.

Systematic sampling of fish eggs at sea was initiated by the German
planktologist Victor Hensen (1895) (Fig. 2) who devised a special net
to catch pelagic fish eggs in a quantitative way.   However, first it
was not so much the estimate of the number of the eggs in a certain sea
area but the description and determination of eggs and larvae which
attracted the interest of marine biologists, particularly in Germany.
Ehrenbaum (1909) (Fig. 3) published a comprehensive account of those
studies which became the standard book for the identification of the

3

early life history stages of marine fish in the northeastern Atlantic until Russell's (1976) recent book on the same subject.

In order to identify the eggs and larvae found in the sea it is often necessary to rear them. Artificial fertilization was done to follow the ontogenesis of identification characters. Already in 1872, Kupffer (1878) fertilized herring eggs and Meyer (1878) reared a few larvae from egg to metamorphosis. It was not until 90 years later that Blaxter (1968) had greater success in rearing herring larvae. The most detailed study of development of plaice eggs in relation to temperature was already done by Apstein (1909).

The early rearing experiments for general natural history studies and for identification were soon followed by mass production of fish larvae in hatcheries. The drastic increase in fishing intensity after the introduction of steam trawlers during the fourth quarter of the nineteenth century had caused a decline in the catch-per-effort of many fish stocks. Fishermen, government authorities, and also scientists believed in a detrimental effect of the fishery on the reproductive potential of the stocks and in a decline in recruitment. Therefore, they proposed artificial production of larvae for restocking. The very good results of stocking lakes with various kinds of fish were an incentive for trying the same in the sea. Fishermen realized that billions of eggs were "wasted" in catches of spawners. They felt that part of those eggs should be saved and brought into hatcheries.

Eggs of all marine species of major economic interest were reared and the yolk sac larvae released in inshore waters. For that purpose, hatcheries were built in many countries, particularly in Britain, Norway, North America, and Japan.

The marine fish hatchery movement of 1880 to 1920, as reported by Shelbourne (1965), can be summarized as follows:

1878 - successful rearing at Gloucester and Kiel, Germany.
1885 - first commercial marine fish hatchery in Woods Hole, Massachusetts, followed by Gloucester Point (1888) and Boothbay Harbor, Maine (1905).
1884 - Norwegian hatcheries in Flødevigen, 1908 - Trondhjemsfjord, Norway.
1893 - Dunbar, Scotland, 1902 - Port Erin, Isle of Man.
1917 - 3×10^9 eggs per annum hatched at the United States east coast hatcheries.
1943-1952 - the three United States east coast hatcheries were closed, much later than most European establishments, with the exception of the still existing station at Flødevigen. In the late 1950's new attempts were started to develop artificial propagation of marine fish for commercial purposes, particularly in Japan and in England (Shelbourne 1964, 1965). Kinne (1977) summarized recent progress in this field in the laboratories of several countries. Until now there are only a few examples for the successful transfer from the experimental to the commercial phase of rearing marine fish larvae.

It took a long time for the marine fishery biologists concerned with those activities to convince themselves and the fishing community of the fact that only under the very special conditions of luxury species

4

in confined habitats is it possible and profitable to restock the sea by artificially reared larvae. However, the mass production of fish larvae in hatcheries and the dispute about its usefulness contributed considerably to the knowledge of the early life history of fish and the development of concepts about the relationship between parent stock, survival of the eggs and larvae, and recruitment.

An egg census was first applied by Hensen and Apstein (1897) in 1895 in the North Sea. In 1909 Buchanan-Wollaston started to estimate the total size of the spawning stock of plaice in the North Sea on the basis of abundance figures of plaice eggs, their temperature-dependent rate of development, data on fecundity of plaice of different sizes, and on the stock composition (Buchanan-Wollaston 1926).

Similar estimates of overall egg production of marine fish stocks were carried out by other workers, particularly Sette (1943) on Atlantic mackerel off the United States Atlantic Coast, Sette and Ahlstrom (1948) on California sardine, Simpson (1951, 1956) again on North Sea plaice, Cushing (1957) on pilchard in the English Channel, and by Japanese workers on sardine and mackerel eggs (Tanaka 1973, 1974).

In 1910, Hjort (Fig. 4) and Lea had shown that the great fluctuations in Norwegian fisheries were at least partly due to differences in year class strength of herring and cod. Hjort (1914) suggested that the earliest larval stages are the most critical period during which later year class strengths are largely determined. That being the case it seemed possible to forecast subsequent year class strength at an early stage well prior to recruitment to the exploited stock. Furthermore, scientists became interested in the causes of differences in survival from year to year. Hjort suggested two major factors influencing early mortality rates: paucity of food during the early larval life and transport by currents into unfavorable areas. The concepts of a short "critical period" in early larval life and its consequences for possible forecasting is not applicable to many fish stocks; in fact, it has been successfully applied in only a few cases (May 1974); in many other species the determination of later year class strength may take place over a much longer period during early life history. However, the crucial role of the pelagic phase was widely accepted and gave the impetus to a great number of field studies and routine programs, so-called egg and larva surveys. Major spawning areas were located and kept under surveillance year after year, and distribution and abundance of fish larvae were correlated with data on environmental factors, e.g., wind, currents, temperature regime, and abundance of food of different sizes. For example, Walford (1938) studied the drift of haddock eggs and larvae at Georges Bank, Buckmann (1950) followed variations in the distribution of herring larvae in the North Sea, and Wiborg (1957) and Dragesund (1970) investigated the transport of cod and herring larvae along the Norwegian Coast in relation to environmental factors. Physical and biological oceanography have made good use of most of the surveys which produce large amounts of hydrographical data and plankton collections. Some types of ichthyoplankton can serve as indicators of water masses and their transport. Later on ichthyoplankton surveys were incorporated in multidisciplinary international investigations, e.g., in the Indian Ocean (IIOE), Tropical Atlantic (ICITA), Western Pacific (CSK), Northern Pacific (NORPAC), and Eastern Tropical Pacific (CINECA), all of which included ichthyoplankton surveys aimed at the identification of fish resources, and which took advantage of the observations made on

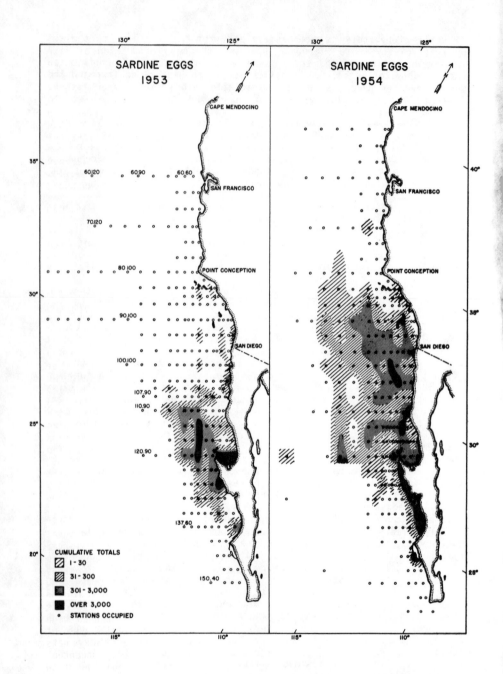

Fig. 5. Distribution and relative abundance of sardine
eggs in 1953 and 1954. Selected station numbers of the
CalCOFI survey are given on the chart for 1953
(Ahlstrom 1965).

the aquatic environment by other disciplines.

Long-term routine ichthyoplankton surveys were largely aimed at an understanding of the causes of fluctuations in year class strength and hence at the provision of a broad and sound basis for fishery forecasts. They rarely met those objectives. However, they revealed the complex relationships of fish eggs and larvae to their abiotic and biotic environment. The surveys also demonstrated more clearly than fishing data the long-term changes in relative abundance of parental stocks and in the predominance of certain species, e.g., the shift from sardine to anchovy in California waters, as described by the largest program of this kind, the California Cooperative Oceanic Fisheries Investigations (CalCOFI), initiated in 1949, and still continued, although on a reduced and modified scale since 1961, as part of the MARMAP program of the U.S. National Marine Fisheries Service. Hundreds of papers describe the results of these surveys which are by far the most extensive studies of fish egg and larva distribution (examples of distribution maps for sardine eggs are shown in Fig. 5). For the different regions of the world FAO has published a review of important publications on surveys and on identification of fish eggs and larvae (Fagetti 1973).

Physiological studies of fish eggs were favored since the 1920's by the hatchery activities. Eggs of salmonids were preferred, as they are large and have long incubation times. Experiments with larvae were held up by the great difficulty of keeping them in aquaria under adequate conditions. Sea-caught larvae rarely survive the manipulation of transfer into the tank and reliable methods for mass rearing of larvae well beyond yolk sac stage were developed only in the last two decades. Sensory physiology, osmoregulation, metabolism, and feeding behavior are the major topics of experimental studies. Work on the food of herring larvae at sea started in the 1920's and was compared with the results of early rearing experiments. Feeding ecology, including size of food taken, daily food requirements, feeding and digestion rates, were only recently studied in the sea and in aquaria. The effect of pollutants on fish eggs and larvae is a new and growing field of physiological research. A summary of the experimental work related to the cultivation of marine fish eggs and larvae is given by Kinne (1977); an annotated bibliography of the same subject was published by May (1971).

Russell (1926) demonstrated that marine fish larvae show diurnal vertical migrations. Studies of the vertical distribution of larvae were continued after the war, and related to feeding and to possible net avoidance. The selectivity of plankton gear is a matter of great concern to everyone engaged in quantitative sampling of fish larvae. Differences in number and size composition of larvae sampled at the same spot by different gear and day and night gave rise to methodological disputes. For a while oblique hauls with encased high speed nets seemed to supersede the classical vertically hauled gear of the type of a Hensen net, at least in Europe. But nowadays large nets towed obliquely or vertically at low speeds are more widely accepted, particularly in international cooperative studies. Depth and flow recordings are added and further environmental data such as temperature and small food plankton are collected simultaneously. However, a simple ichthyoplankton net with a reliable closing device for sampling in selected depth zones still does not exist.

Most recently the need of integrated studies in the survival of ichthyoplankton is widely recognized. Particularly under the MARMAP program of the U.S. National Marine Fisheries Service (NMFS) and related programs in Canada and Germany there is an attempt to link together:

      a)   Laboratory experiments on ecologically important aspects of the physiology of fish eggs and larvae, including studies on the effects of "pre-natal" and "post-natal" application of sublethal doses of pollutants.

      b)   Experiments on survival, grazing, and growth of larvae in large bags or netting suspended in inshore waters.

      c)   Microscale studies on the life history and biological impact of patches of fish larvae in the sea, including studies in temporal and spatial co-occurrence of larvae with their predators and food organisms. Macroscale observations on distribution and abundance of ichthyoplankton in relation to water mass distribution and plankton composition in order to show differences between years and areas.

The results of the various approaches should become the theoretical and factual basis of descriptive and predictive models on the population dynamics of ichthyoplankton and its relation to the juvenile and adult fish stocks.

CONCLUSIONS

The history of a century of studies on fish eggs and larvae can be divided roughly into two major periods of about equal duration: a) Nonquantitative sampling at sea for studies in identification, life history, and overall distribution of eggs and early larvae. Rearing work in hatcheries for the description of developmental stages. b) Quantitative surveys for estimates of abundance as a measure of parent stock size and subsequent recruitment. Studies on the ecology of fish eggs and larvae at sea and experimental contributions to the physiological ecology of the early life history stages.

Although the aims of the studies often were not clearly defined, four major objectives can be distinguished (Hempel 1974):

Objective 1: General knowledge about fish eggs and larvae per se, morphogenesis, physiology, behavior, taxonomy, systematics, and zoogeography. The development of morphological structures, behavioral patterns, and physiological functions in fish larvae is of particular biological interest in view of the drastic changes from a passively or almost passively floating egg and yolk sac larva to a freely moving, predatory fish larva and later to, for example, a schooling pelagic herring or a demersal halibut.

Objective 2: Ichthyoplankton is sometimes an important element of aquatic ecosystems. The role of fish eggs and larvae in the food web is to be studied. Early stages of fish may serve as indicators of pollution as they seem to be more sensitive than older fish. So far only a few authors have applied the ecosystem approach to ichthyoplankton.

Objective 3: To rear fish eggs and larvae is an important prerequisite for aquaculture including selective breeding, for toxicity tests, physiological and genetical studies, and for identification of

8

undescribed or poorly identifiable eggs and larvae.

Objective 4: The knowledge of fish populations and their optimum exploitation can be augmented by using fish eggs and larvae as indicators for the existence and size of parent stock and future recruitment. They should help to differentiate between man-made and natural effects on fish stocks and to detect long-term trends in distribution, composition, and abundance of fish populations.

Experimental work in laboratories and hatcheries, together with small-scale field studies, are mainly concerned with objectives 1 and 3; large-scale ichthyoplankton surveys are oriented toward objective 4 but contribute also to zoogeography and ecosystem analysis.

The majority of modern studies on fish eggs and larvae is made by fishery-oriented institutions, but most of them cannot easily be called applied research in a narrow sense. Already at an early stage of fishery biology, it was understood that a broad knowledge of taxonomy, biology, and ecology of the early life history stages of fish is essential for answering certain practical questions, particularly with regard to the exploitation of fish populations. Studies of fish eggs and larvae provide unique opportunities to link pure and applied research and to bring into close contact ichthyologists, physiologists, ecologists, and oceanographers.

LITERATURE ON MARINE FISH EGGS AND LARVAE

The literature on our subject is very widely scattered. The majority of papers on the early life history stages of fish is found in the journals of fishery biology and marine biology. Several important contributions are to be found in more general journals and conference proceedings on zoology and ecology. Many findings of great interest, particularly in methodology, are buried in the "grey" literature of internal reports and mimeographed papers for national and international meetings. It is virtually impossible to keep track of those publications. The list of references given at the end of this paper is highly selective by covering just that fraction of the literature used in preparation and revision of the text.

There is no textbook on the early life history of fish and ecology of ichthyoplankton in relation to fishery biology. However, useful reviews for certain fields have been published by various authors. A selection of those reviews is listed below. The state of knowledge was furthermore summarized at a number of symposia dealing with the early life history of fish and its relevance to fishery biology. The published proceedings of four symposia were extensively used in preparing the lecture notes, as many of their contributions are useful summaries of the work carried out in the various laboratories and institutions.

REVIEWS

Physiology and Development

Blaxter, J. H. S., and F. G. T. Holliday. 1963. The behaviour and
    physiology of herring and other clupeoids. Pages 261-393 *in* F.

S. Russell, ed. Adv. Mar. Biol., Vol. 1. New York, London.

Hoar, W. S., and D. J. Randall, eds. 1969. Fish physiology. Vol. 3.
   New York, Acad. Press. 483 pp.

Ichthyoplankton in Relation to Fisheries

Simpson, A. C. 1956. The pelagic phase. Pages 207-250 *in* M. Graham,
   ed. Sea fisheries, their investigation in the United Kingdom.
   Arnold, London.

Reproduction and Recruitment

Cushing, D. H. 1973. Recruitment and parent stock in fishes.
   Washington Sea Grant Publication 73-1. 197 pp.

Rearing and Aquaculture

Kinne, O. 1977. Cultivation: Fishes. Pages 968-1035 *in* O. Kinne,
   ed. Mar. Ecol. 3(2). Chichester, J. Wiley.

General Description

Russell, F. S. 1976. The eggs and planktonic stages of British marine
   fishes. London, Acad. Press. 524 pp.

Methodology of Ichthyoplankton Surveys

Hempel, G., ed. 1973. Fish egg and larvae surveys (Contributions to a
   manual). FAO Fish. Tech. Paper No. 122. 82 pp.

Smith, P. E., and S. L. Richardson. 1977. Standard techniques for
   pelagic fish egg and larva surveys. FAO Fish. Tech. Paper No. 175.
   100 pp.

Symposia

Symposium on larval fish biology, Lake Arrowhead, California, 29-31
   October 1963, R. Lasker, Convener. 1965. CalCOFI Reps.
   10:12-152.

Symposium on the biology of early stages and recruitment mechanisms of
   herring, Charlottenlund, Denmark, 25-28 September 1968. A.
   Saville, Convener. 1964. Rapp. P.-V. Reun., ICES, Vol. 160.
   205 pp.

Symposium on fish stocks and recruitment, Aarhus, Denmark, 7-10 July
   1971, B. B. Parrish, Convener. 1973. Rapp. P.-V. Réun., ICES,
   Vol. 164. 372 pp.

International Symposium on the early life history of fish, Oban,
   Scotland, 17-23 May 1973. J. H. S. Blaxter, Convener. 1974. J.
   H. S. Blaxter, ed. The early life history of fish. Springer,
   Berlin, Heidelberg, New York. 765 pp.

PRODUCTION OF EGGS

The role of reproduction in fish--as in all organisms--is to perpetuate the species, to ensure genetic mixing as well as adaption by selection, and to allow the development of new species by mutations. Pelagic eggs and larvae, produced in very great numbers, ensure the necessary flexibility in distribution of fish in a changing environment and give the basis for selection. All fish reproduce sexually, and most of them are bisexual. Hermaphroditism occurs regularly in some serranids where even self-fertilization is reported. Other serranids are protandric hermaphrodites. In several other groups of teleosts, some few specimens with both types of sex glands were found. Those fish might even be functional hermaphrodites, i.e., producing eggs and sperm at the same time. However, in most species of teleosts hermaphroditism is a rare abnormality. In several species embryonic development can be triggered by external factors without spermatozoa. With few exceptions, those embryos die before the end of incubation period.

DEVELOPMENT OF GONADS AND EGG CELLS

Morphology of reproductive organs, and physiology and morphology of eggs and sperm will be described very briefly, being somewhat outside the scope of the present lecture notes. Comments relate particularly to fish which produce pelagic eggs. For more detailed information reference is made to Hoar and Randall, "Physiology of fishes," Vol. 3, and to textbooks of comparative anatomy and ichthyology (e.g., Lagler et al. 1962; Harder 1964). The gonads are originally paired, and remain so in most species. They hang on mesenteries in the upper part of the body cavity.

The testes are composed of follicles which contain the developing spermatozoa; they look reddish when immature and become creamy-white in the process of ripening. Their content is then flocculent. The ovaries look like white or red strings in immature fish and turn golden

11

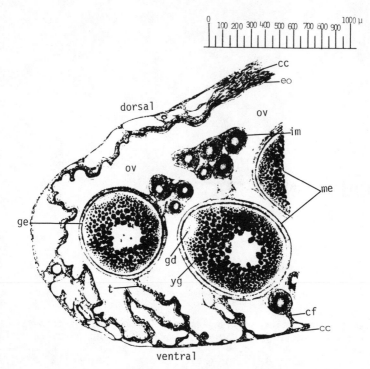

Fig. 6a. Cross-section of the ovary of a pike (*Esox lucius*) (Harder 1964). Abbreviations are: cc - connective tissue capsule, ou - oviduct, eo - epithelium of oviduct, ge - germinal epithelium, t - transition of ge into eo, cf - connective tissue folds of ovarial stroma, me - mature eggs, im - immature eggs, gd - germinal disc, yd - yolk granula.

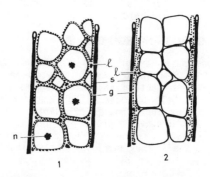

Fig. 6b. Cross-section of part of a herring ovary: 1) before ovulation, septa (s) with eggs between them; 2) after ovulation. The eggs lie free in the lumen of the ovary. Granulosa walls (g) and young oocytes (ℓ) have withdrawn toward the septa, nucleus (n) (Polder 1961).

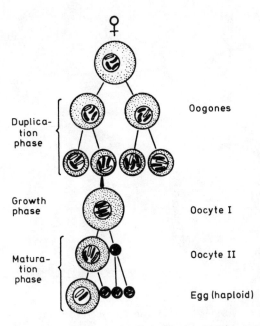

Fig. 7. Oogenesis in fish (Harder 1964).

or reddish golden when ripening. Finally, shortly before extrusion the
individual eggs turn transparent and become visible through the ovary
wall.

In most higher bony fishes the caudal part of the ovarian capsule
continues as an oviduct, so that the ripe eggs can pass from the ovary
directly into the egg canal. In sharks and other chondrichthyans the
gonad is not directly connected with the oviduct. In salmonids the
oviduct is missing or greatly reduced. The eggs fall from the ovary
into the body cavity and exit through pores adjacent to the rectal and
urinary openings.

The ovary wall consists of an external layer of connective tissue, a
pigment layer, and a muscle layer. These layers are not distinctly
separated from each other. The lumen of the ovarial sac is partly
filled with vascular connective tissue (stroma) which is folded and
rich in elastic tissue and muscles. The stroma is attached to the
ovary wall; the surface of the stroma is covered by germinal
epithelium (Figs. 6a, b).

The oogones arise in the germinal epithelium from primordial sex cells,
pass through mitotic divisions, and develop to Class I oocytes which
look transparent, as originally no yolk is stored in the oocyte
(Fig. 7). The oocyte becomes surrounded by small epithelial cells to
form the ovarian follicles. The epithelial cells grow in size and
number; they form a glandular granulosa. Between the granulosa and the
oocyte there is the noncellular transparent zona pellucida. The
granulosa is responsible for the deposition of yolk in the oocyte
Class I and for removal of the yolk in atretic oocytes degenerating
before ovulation (Fig. 8). The ripe oocyte is surrounded by a thick

13

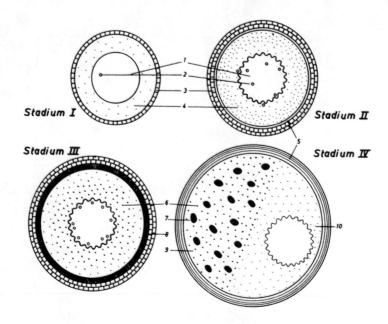

Fig. 8. Development of an oocyte (Gotting 1961): 1,
nucleus; 2, nucleolus; 3, follicle; 4, plasma; 5,
cortical layers; 6,7, yolk particles; 8, cortex radiata;
9, vegetative pole; 10, animal pole.

periviteline membrane. It consists of an inner amorphous membrane
which is perforated by fine channels. Fingerlike extrusions
(microvilli) of the oocyte of about 0, 1 μ in diameter reach through
the channels. The very large surface of the microvilli is responsible
for the exchange of matter between the oocyte and the follicle cells
surrounding the oocyte. Yolk is deposited on the young oocyte either
around the nucleus or at the periphery. When ovulation takes place,
the nucleus migrates from the center to the periphery together with the
surrounding plasma, while the yolk concentrates in the other
hemisphere.

The increase in dry matter and changes in the proportion of the major
constituents of the egg--protein, water, ash--were described by Milroy
(1908), Bruce (1924), and Ehlebracht (1973) for herring and by Mengi
(1963) for Baltic cod. The very young transparent oocytes are high in
water content; their protein later increases by incorporation of the
yolk (Fig. 9). Finally, the egg becomes transparent again by the water
uptake. These changes are reflected in the water content of the oocyte:
in Baltic cod water content decreases from about 84% to 63% in the
course of vitellogenesis. Just before spawning it rises again to 88%.
At this stage no further protein is stored in the oocyte. Considerable
changes occur in the concentration of certain amino acids and peptides
in the course of the development of the eggs. The final composition of
the egg protein differs from the maternal tissue (Bussmann 1978).
Certain amino acids and peptides are rapidly incorporated, thereby
depleting the muscle tissue of the mother (Flüchter and Trommsdorf
1974).

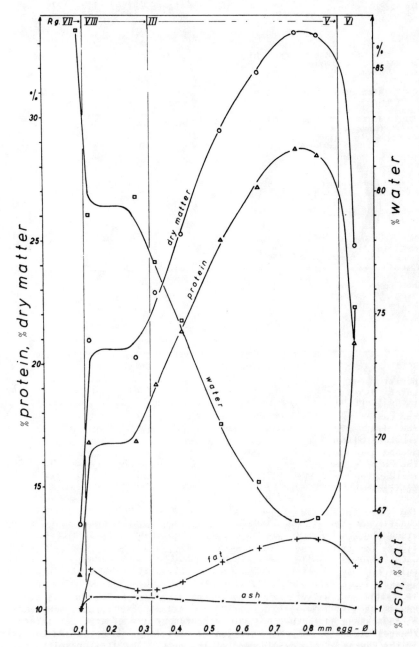

Fig. 9. The increase in dry matter and changes in the proportions of the main constituents of the egg (Ehlebracht 1973). Dry matter (0) is the sum of protein + fat + ash; Ø = diameter of the egg expressed in mm; Rg = maturity stages VII and VIII and III - VI.

Table 1. Ovarian development and maturity stages (after Hilge 1975, 1977).

	Maier 1906	Naumow 1956	Sivertsen 1937	Hilge 1977
Ovary translucent, oocytes transparent, not recognizable to the naked eye	I juvenile	I juvenile	I immature	I juvenile
Ovary opaque, small crystal-clear oocytes	II rest	II preparation		
Ovary and oocytes not transparent, oocytes at the beginning of vitellogenesis	III preparation	III ripening		II ripening
Ovary not transparent, oocytes filled with yolk	IV crowding	IV ripe	II ripening	
Ovary fills body cavity, few diaphanous ripe eggs	V elongation	V spawning	III ripe	
Ovary translucent, eggs transparent	VI ripe			III running
Ovary shortened, translucent opaque, slimy content, transparent and whitish eggs	VII half-spent	VI spent	IV spent	IV spent
Ovary opaque, ovary walls slack, residual eggs	VIII spent			

In the spent ovary the water content of the remaining eggs is similar to the early stages of oocytes. The mature egg in herring and cod contains very little carbohydrates and also only 2-3% fat. The fat content in the body tissues of spring spawning Baltic herring decreases from about 17% during the feeding period in autumn to 2-3% at the end of the spawning period. Most of the body fat is used for metabolism rather than for storage in the egg.

MATURITY STAGES

Determination of the stage of maturity of gonads is an important routine method to describe the reproductive cycle and to relate the individual fish--or more often a group of fishes--to a certain stock as a reproductive unit. Furthermore, it describes the percentage of juvenile fish in a given population. When working up large samples of fish at sea and at the fish market it is impossible to analyze the developmental stages of ovaries and testes under the microscope. The macroscopic inspection of the gonads must suffice. In fish with one short clear-cut spawning season per year there are indeed a number of stages discernible by the naked eye: resting stage--the ovary is very thin and similar to the ovary of an immature fish, although the wall of the ovary is thicker in repeat spawners than in recruit spawners approaching first maturity. The resting stage often covers the larger part of the year. The various preparatory stages are of different duration depending on the spawning season in relation to the annual feeding and temperature cycle. In the final preparatory phase the eggs are so large and filled with yolk that they become easily visible through the ovary wall. When ovulation takes place, the eggs become transparent by the intake of body fluid. Then the eggs are ripe.

16

Table 2.   Scale of gonadal development (maturity stages) of herring, as adopted by the International Council for the Exploration of the Sea in 1962 (from Harden Jones 1968).

Stage

I.   Virgin herring. Gonads very small, thread-like, 2-3 mm broad; ovaries wine-red; testes whitish or grey-brown.

II.   Virgin herring with small sexual organs. The height of ovaries and testes about 3-8 mm; eggs not visible to naked eye but can be seen with magnifying glass; ovaries a bright red color; testes a reddish-grey color.

III.   Gonads occupying about half of the ventral cavity. Breadth of sexual organs between 1 and 2 cm; eggs small but can be distinguished with naked eye; ovaries orange; testes reddish-grey or greyish.

IV.   Gonads almost as long as body cavity. Eggs larger, varying in size, opaque; ovaries orange or pale yellow; testes whitish.

V.   Gonads fill body cavity. Eggs large, round; some transparent; ovaries yellowish; testes milk-white; eggs and sperm do not flow, but sperm can be extruded by pressure.

VI.   Ripe gonads. Eggs transparent; testes white; eggs and sperm flow freely.

VII.   Spent herring. Gonads baggy and bloodshot; ovaries empty or containing only a few residual eggs; testes may contain remains of sperm.

VIII.   Recovering spents. Ovaries and testes firm and larger than virgin herring in Stage II; eggs not visible to naked eye; walls of gonads striated; blood vessels prominent; gonads wine-red color. (This stage passes into Stage III.)

After spawning the ovary is bloody, containing some unshed eggs which will be reabsorbed during the recovery phase, which leads to a new resting stage.

For standardized description of maturity stages various scales have been proposed either for individual species such as herring and cod or for all species which have a distinct spawning season (Table 1). Hjort's scale for herring became the basis for the recommendations by the International Council for the Exploration of the Sea ("ICES scale," Table 2). It is--as are all others--partly artificial, as it cuts the more-or-less continuous development of maturation into sections which are not equal in duration and which are sometimes difficult to define in a reproducible manner. Scales with fewer stages have been proposed by various authors. A recent one by Hilge (1975, 1977) is based on four "natural" stages in ovary development lumping together stages II-IV, VII-VIII of the ICES scale into two stages, II and IV, respectively.

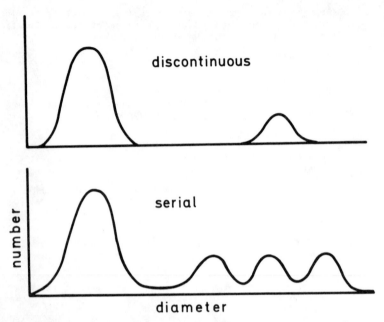

Fig. 10. Differences in size distributions of oocytes of discontinuous and serial spawners.

The rate of growth of the gonads may differ even within species, depending on spawning season of its various races. In spring spawning herring the early stages are much prolonged, while the final stages which coincide with the good feeding season are very short. The duration of the spawning season is rather different in fish living under different environmental regimes. In cold water species a certain number of oocytes grow simultaneously, leading to a single spawning act per year. The size frequency curve of oocytes in cold water fish shows a distinct bimodal distribution, with one maximum consisting of maturing oocytes for the season and the other consisting of oogonia and minute resting oocytes for later years. In cod it seems possible to distinguish between several different size groups of resting oocytes which represent the spawning potential of the female for up to 5 successive years (Hilge 1975). Particularly salmoniform fish spawn only once in their life. Bakke and Bjørke (1971) observed natural mass mortality of capelin on the Norwegian spawning grounds.

Production of ripe eggs in an individual fish may be limited either to a short period of the year--discontinuous spawning at a distinct spawning season--or may extend over a major part of the year, during which a series of spawnings will take place. The latter, serial type of spawning is common in fishes living in low latitudes, while discontinuous spawning is typical for fishes of temperate and cold waters, where within a short spawning season the fish extrude all their eggs in one single batch or spawn repeatedly at intervals of some days. Discontinuous and serial spawners differ markedly in the size pattern of their oocytes, size distribution of oocytes in serial spawners being polymodal (Fig. 10).

Fig. 11. Types of spherical eggs
(after Russell 1976): 1,2 large
eggs, large perivitelline space
with or without oil globule; 3,4
total segmentation of yolk with or
without oil globule total segmentation of yolk; 5-7 peripheral
segmentation with many oil globules
in clusters or randomly distributed
with only one oil globule; 8-10
unsegmented yolk (most common type)
with many, one or no oil globule.

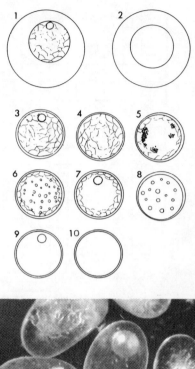

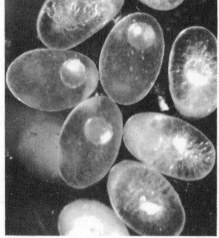

Fig. 12. Anchovy eggs (photograph
by Nellen).

MORPHOLOGY OF THE EGG AND ITS USE
FOR SPECIES IDENTIFICATION

Identification of newly spawned pelagic fish eggs is often impossible.
A number of characters may help to differentiate between eggs of
different species spawning simultaneously: shape and size of the egg,
structure of the egg shell (chorion), pigmentation of the yolk, and
number and size of oil globules. Most fish eggs are spherical
(Fig. 11). Oval eggs occur in various families including engraulids
(Fig. 12), minnows, cichlids, and gobies. The eggs of flying fishes
and some others have adhesive filaments. Tendrils and other appendages
anchor demersal eggs of various elasmobranchs and teleosts to the
bottom or to plants.

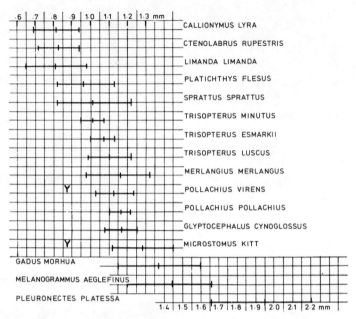

Fig. 13. Eggs of fishes of the northeastern Atlantic (after Simpson 1956). Diameter of eggs without oil globules; Y indicates black pigment develops on the yolk [not included are *Hippoglossoides platessoides* (diameter 1.4-3.5 mm) and *Hippoglossus hippoglossus* (3.0-4.2 mm)].

Marine fish eggs are normally about 1 mm in diameter. In a few species egg diameter ranges between 1.5-2.6 mm. Demersal eggs and eggs of freshwater fish tend to be larger, particularly in salmonids. The largest of all fish eggs are found in elasmobranchs.

Diameter is an important measure for the species identification of eggs wherever, in a given area and season, different species of fish spawn simultaneously. Already in 1911, ICES published identification sheets for the fish eggs of the northeastern Atlantic. Simpson (1956) gave a graphical presentation of size differences (Figs. 13, 14, 15).

The chorion is normally smooth, but a hexagonal sculpturing occurs in some species. It is rather thick and sometimes horny in benthic eggs where sticky hairs also occur, e.g., as in *Belone*. In egg-laying sharks and skates the eggs have particularly horny shells of very high mechanical resistance. In eggs with parental care the egg shell is often very thin. The scanning electron microscope reveals that the surface of the chorion has a microstructure with a characteristic pattern of diagnostic value. However, the method is too cumbersome to be used as a routine method in fishery biology.

Within the newly fertilized eggs three zones can be recognized: The spherical yolk mass which normally appears homogenous, but which in some species is peripherally or totally divided into segmental

20

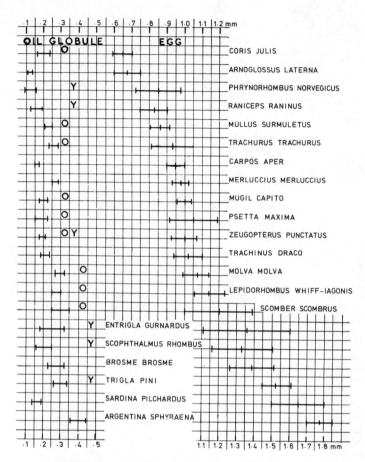

Fig. 14. Eggs of fishes of the northeastern Atlantic
(after Simpson 1956). Eggs with a single oil globule.
Diameter of egg and of oil globule.

partitions. Oil globules are found in the yolk of many species:
either a large single globule in the yolk lying opposite the nucleus or
several small globules evenly distributed in the yolk or in clusters in
which many small globules merge into a single large one. The yolk is
surrounded by a thin protoplasmic film, the periblast, with the nucleus
of the egg cell in a lens-shaped thickening where the blastoderm will
develop. Between periblast and chorion there is a narrow space filled
with water, the perivitelline space. In a few species the perivitelline space is very wide, e.g., *Sardina pilchardus* and *Hippoglossoides
platessoides*.

As shown in Figs. 11, 13, and 14, size and number of oil globules and
structure of the yolk supplement egg size as means for identification
of eggs.

In certain species black and yellowish-green pigment are found on the
yolk, oil globules, and later on the embryo. Only in a few species do

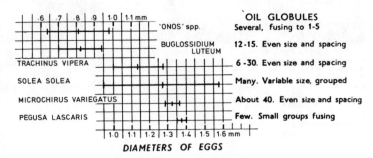

Fig. 15. Eggs of fishes of the northeastern Atlantic (after Simpson 1956). Diameter of eggs with more than one oil globule: *Onos* spp. has several oil globules fusing to 1-5. Oil globules of even size and spacing are found in *Buglossidium luteum* (12-15), *Microchirus variegatus* (ca.40), *Trachinus vipera* (6-30). Many grouped oil globules in *Solea solea*, a few fusing in *Pegusa lascaris*.

the yolk or the chorion show characteristic structures. Identification becomes easier at later stages of embryogenesis when the shape of the embryo, the timing of the eye pigmentation, as well as the pigmentation pattern of embryo and yolk, provide additional information; but all this might still be insufficient in areas in which many species spawn at the same time.

FECUNDITY

The term fecundity refers to the number of ripe eggs produced by a female in one spawning season or year (absolute fecundity). Sometimes the term is also used for the total number of eggs produced during the average lifespan of a female, the lifetime fecundity which is always much smaller than the original number of small oocytes, most of which become reabsorbed at intermediate stages or never ripen. Relative fecundity is the number of eggs produced in a season per unit somatic weight of the fish.

Both the number of small oocytes and the proportion of ripe eggs vary greatly from species to species and even between races of one species. The annual fecundity depends also largely on size and age of the fish and on its nutritional condition. Already Fulton (1891) described the increase in absolute fecundity with fish size and the great differences in relative fecundity between marine fish species of Scottish waters.

Measuring Fecundity

Determination of fecundity is usually carried out by counting the ripening or ripe oocytes prior to ovulation. The procedure is either by counting one or more aliquots of the ovary under the dissection microscope or by means of placing the total content of the ovary into an automatic egg counting apparatus, in which all oocytes above a given size give a signal, when passing through a light beam or an electrical field.

Ovaries for egg counting are usually fixed and treated in Gilson's fluid to harden the eggs and separate them from the gonadal connective tissue. The determination is based on the assumption that the number of ripening oocytes does not change after stage III of the ICES scale. This has been tested for North Sea herring. In fish with more continuous egg production fecundity estimates are far more difficult and require detailed knowledge of the reproductive cycle.

Genetic Differences in Relative Fecundity

Fecundity figures range from a few eggs in elasmobranchs to several millions in marine gadoids and in oceanic pelagic fish like *Molva* (Table 3). In general, highest fecundity is found in fish which spawn pelagic eggs, intermediate numbers of thousands to ten-thousands are produced by fish which lay their eggs at the bottom or on vegetation, while low numbers are typical for fish which take care of their brood.

Table 3. Fecundity, egg size, and length at hatching of some fishes (Blaxter 1969).

	Eggs per year	Diameter of egg (mm)	Length of larva at hatching (mm)
Ling (*Molva molva*)	$2-3 \times 10^7$	1.0-1.1	3-3.5
Cod (*Gadus morhua*)	$2-9 \times 10^6$	1.1-1.6	4
Plaice (*Pleuronectes platessa*)	$2 \times 10^4 - 3 \times 10^5$	1.7-2.2	6-7
Mackerel (*Scomber scombrus*)	4×10^5	1.0-1.4	3-4
Herring (*Clupea harengus*)	$5 \times 10^3 - 2 \times 10^5$	0.9-1.7	5-8
Salmon (*Salmo salar*)	$10^2 - 10^4$	5-6	15-25
Smelt (*Osmerus eperlanus*)	$5 \times 10^3 - 5 \times 10^4$	0.9	4-6
Sturgeon (*Acipenser sturio*)	10^6	-	9
Carp (*Cyprinus carpio*)	$2-5 \times 10^5$	0.9-1.6	5-6
Spotted dogfish (*Scyliorhinus caniculus*)	2-20	65 (length)	100
Blenny* (*Zoarces viviparus*)	20-300	-	35-40 at birth
Redfish* (*Sebastes viviparus*)	$1-3 \times 10^4$	-	5-8 at birth
Spur dogfish (*Squalus acanthias*)	2-7	24-32	240-310 at birth

*Viviparous or ovoviviparous.

An exception is the ovoviviparous *Sebastes* which extrudes more than 100,000 young larvae.

Racial differences in fecundity were described for several species, e.g., herring (summarized by Parrish and Saville 1965; Schopka 1971), various flatfish (Bagenal 1966; Kandler and Pirwitz 1957), and cod (Botros 1962, Schopka 1971). While Norwegian spring-spawning herring of 27 cm total length have only 23,000 eggs, Baltic autumn spawners of the same length average 78,000 eggs.

Effects of Size and Age of Fish on Fecundity

Fulton (1891) first found that larger fish of the same species have more eggs than smaller fish. Since then the relationship of fecundity with size and age of the fish has been described by several formulae. A review of the literature was recently given by Schopka (1971). It is still an open question which factor related to body size of the fish finally determines fecundity: Does the germinal epithelium grow proportional to the second power of the fish length, as other surfaces do, or is it folded to an extent that the volume of the gonad is the limiting factor? Does the ovary itself grow in proportion to the body weight of the fish? Is egg size independent of the size of the mother? To what extent is the relationship between body size and fecundity masked by differences in age and condition of the mother? In Fig. 16 fecundity-length relationships are shown for 10 species of fish of very different biology. The slope is rather similar while fecundity per unit length is different. In most cases the increase in fecundity (F) with body length (L) can be described by the formula by Raitt (1933).

$$F = (a)\,(L^b).$$

The best fit is often near L^3, i.e., increase in fecundity is almost proportional to the fish weight. Schopka (1971) found values between $L^{2.8}$ and $L^{3.5}$ in various populations of cod (*Gadus morhua*), but in herring (*Clupea harengus*) fecundity increases at a faster rate than body weight, the data fit curves of $L^{3.4}$ to $L^{6.8}$ depending on the race, on average $L^{3.9}$. The racial differences in the exponent of L were not statistically significant. There is always a great amount of variability in fecundity even between fish of the same population, size, and age.

In most cases the number of fish investigated is too small to separate statistically the effect of age from the effect of body size on fecundity. However, Schopka (1971) confirmed for Norwegian herring that older fish of a given size group produce more eggs. This was independent of the fish being a first-time spawner or a repeat spawner. Similar findings have been reported for various other fish (in review by Bagenal 1973). On the other hand, in populations living under extremely poor conditions of a short feeding period, fish with no previous spawning may have a higher relative fecundity than repeat spawners which did not make full use of the short feeding season due to the previous spawning (e.g., White Sea herring, Anokhina 1963).

Egg Production of a Stock

If fecundity is in linear proportion to the weight of the fish, i.e., number of eggs per g of mature female (relative fecundity) is constant

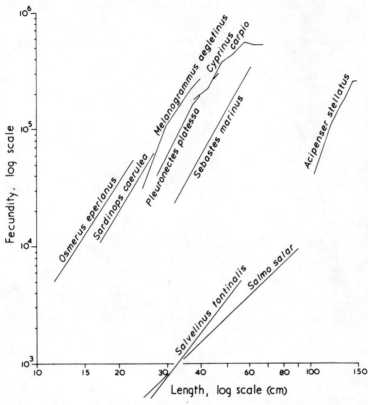

Fig. 16. Fecundity and body length in some fish species (Blaxter 1969).

over a wide range of fish sizes, then the constant (a) in the above formula serves as a direct measure for the comparison of fecundity between races.

Under the same conditions, estimating total egg production of a stock (population fecundity) is easy if total weight of females is known. If $b = 3$, size composition of the stock has no effect on the total egg production. If, however, fecundity (F) increases with a power of L higher than 3, a stock of large (and old) fish produces far more eggs than a spawning stock of the same total weight but consisting mainly of small fish. This implies that heavily fished stocks of herring produce considerably less eggs than expected from the weight of the stock (Schopka and Hempel 1973). This may have considerable consequences on potential recruitment to the stock, particularly if fecundity in first-time spawners (recruit/spawners) is even lower than to be expected from the overall relationship of egg number to body weight. Such low reproduction in recruits has been suggested by various authors, but was not confirmed by Schopka (1971) for cod and herring when comparing fish of the same size and age.

Variations in Fecundity

Variation in the egg production of a fish population may have several different causes, which have been discussed by Bagenal (1963). Size of the parental stock and the age structure are obvious factors which increase from year to year and, on a more long-term basis, influence total population fecundity through earlier gonad maturation and higher age-specific fecundity. Relative fecundity is affected by feeding conditions. This has been confirmed in experiments by Scott (1962) and Bagenal (1969) in rainbow trout and brown trout, in field observation by Anoknina (1960, 1971) on Baltic and White Sea herring, and by Schopka (1971) on cod. The cause is presumably increased follicular atresia, as shown by Scott (1962) for rainbow trout. Several authors pointed to an inverse relationship between population density and number of eggs found in the sea. I am not convinced that this is due to presumed poorer feeding conditions because of intraspecific competition for food, particularly in cases where individual growth is not affected by high stock density.

EGG SIZE

On one hand the size of the egg determines the size and yolk reserves of the larvae and hence survival to a certain extent. On the other hand the total amount of egg substance produced by a female of a given size must be limited and therefore large eggs mean fewer eggs per female, i.e., lower fecundity, and hence fewer offspring if survival rate were independent of larval size (Svardson 1949). Unfortunately fecundity and the size of the ripe egg cannot be measured in one and the same specimen as in most cases fecundity is counted prior to spawning in order to avoid underestimates because of losses by partial spawning. So far surprisingly little attention has been given to variation in egg size, except for several studies on salmonid eggs.

For 16 species of North Sea fish Bagenal (1963) listed the differences in volume between the largest and smallest eggs as estimated from egg diameters published by Ehrenbaum. In most species the largest eggs have two to three times the volume of the smallest ones. The significance of those differences is poorly understood.

In general the positive correlation with fish size seems weaker in highly fecund marine fish than in salmonids and in *Tilapia* where within a species egg size may vary by a factor of four with size of the mother (Peters 1963). Oosthuizen and Daan (1974) did not find an effect of mother size on North Sea cod eggs. In herring, the increase of egg size with size and age of the mother is rather spurious (Schopka 1971).

There is a relationship between egg size and environmental conditions. Flounder (*Platichthys flesus*) eggs are larger under brackish water conditions than in full seawater (Solemdal 1967). This difference, however, is at least partly due to the higher water content of the eggs in brackish water and is therefore not reflected in the dry weight. On the other hand, cod eggs (dry weight) are smaller in the Baltic than off Iceland and in the North Sea (Schopka 1971). Condition factor of the mother and egg size is negatively correlated in cod and in brook trout, well-fed fish producing more but smaller eggs. In White Sea herring lean fish produce on an average larger eggs which vary much in size. Nikolsky (1969) assumes that the insufficient nutrition of the ovary might be the cause of variability in egg size.

Comparison between species (Table 3) and populations shows also that the size of the egg and of the newly hatched larva is negatively correlated with fecundity. A close inverse relationship between egg size and egg number was found within a given size group of mouth-brooding *Tilapia* populations (Peters 1963). Even in fish with pelagic eggs the production of large eggs with considerable yolk supply and large initial size of the larvae can be considered as a kind of maternal care for the individual offspring, while a high number of small eggs can be considered as a protective measure to ensure survival of the species against high egg and larval mortality, particularly by predation. This argument has been used in the interpretation of fecundity differences between various herring races, spawning at different seasons and with the larvae facing different conditions (Hempel and Blaxter 1967). Herring spawning in winter to early spring produce large eggs in low numbers, summer-autumn spawners much smaller eggs in high quantity (Fig. 17). The general validity of this hypothesis has to be tested by comparing seasonal or geographical races of other fish hatching under different conditions of feeding and predation. In cod and most other fish of northern waters which extend their spawning over some weeks, egg size decreases gradually over the season (Bagenal 1971, 1973). Pilchard spawn occurs off Plymouth all year round, but eggs are considerably larger and are richer in yolk and oil during winter than in summer (Southward and Demir 1974).

EGG MASS

The total dry weight of all ripe eggs produced by a female during one spawning season is called egg mass. It is usually calculated as the product of absolute fecundity and egg size. The ratio of egg mass to body weight is a measure of the reproductive strain, i.e., the total input of a fish of a given size into gonad development (another high expenditure of energy is the spawning migration). This ratio is

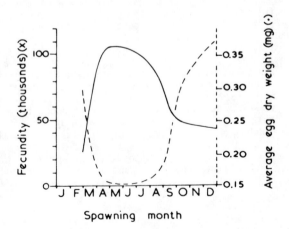

Fig. 17. Egg weight (——) and fecundity (-----) in herring races, spawning in western European waters and in the Baltic in different seasons (Blaxter 1969).

different between species. However, the amount of data in the literature concerning egg mass ratios is rather small considering the physiological and ecological importance of this data. In terms of fresh weight ovaries make up normally 10-25% of body weight, according to Royce (1972). Cod has a ratio of 1 : 4 for egg mass to weight of fish (without gonads); in herring the ratio varies from 1 : 3 in Baltic herring to 1 : 4 in Norwegian herring.

The ratio between body weight and egg mass changes with growth of the fish in accordance with the allometric increase in fecundity. If egg size also increases with size of the mother the increase in egg mass is even higher. In herring this spawning expenditure increases faster than somatic body weight (Fig. 18a). This is particularly the case in Baltic herring which start spawning at a very small size and reach a final length not much above the maturation size of Norwegian herring which has a much slower increase in egg mass. In Baltic herring, but also in North Sea herring, the spawning expenditure per body weight is not only very high at an early start but increases so fast that somatic growth is much reduced compared with Norwegian herring which is more economical in its spawning expenditure. However, the higher somatic growth and longer life span of Norwegian herring will easily compensate for the lower egg mass per unit body weight and year, if the fishery permits the fish to grow sufficiently long (Fig. 18b).

SUMMARY

The development of the egg cell can be summarized as follows: in the juvenile ovary primary sex cells develop into oogonia which divide by mitosis. Then certain oogonia pass through a preparatory phase for meiosis; their nucleus is very large compared to the plasma but the cell grows slowly. Those Class I oocytes become surrounded by the two-layered follicle. Afterwards the oocyte has a great intake of yolk (mainly protein, little fat, almost no carbohydrates) and develops a strong perivitelline membrane which is penetrated by microvilli of the oocyte, establishing close nutritional contacts with the follicle. At ovulation the follicle ruptures and the egg takes up body fluid through the perivitelline membrane. The outer egg membrane, the chorion, develops rapidly at this stage.

Both number and size of eggs and consequently egg mass are specific characters of species and races; they are related to differences in size and age at maturation, adult growth rate, and longevity. Egg size and number are inversely related. The ratio may vary within species depending on spawning season. Fecundity is affected by environmental factors (particularly through the feeding status of the mother). The increase in fecundity with body weight is much larger than the increase in egg size. A direct effect of age--independent of growth--on fecundity and egg size is difficult to detect. There is some evidence of an inverse relationship between population density and fecundity resulting in stabilization of population size (Bagenal 1973).

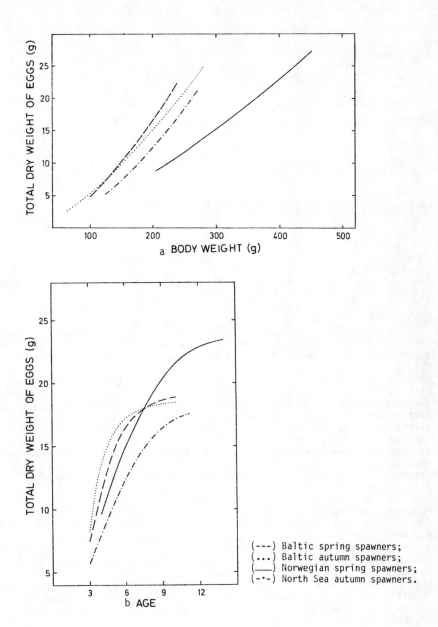

Fig. 18. Total egg mass and body weight (a) or age (b) in four herring races of the northeastern Atlantic (Schopka 1971).

29

SPAWNING AND FERTILIZATION

All Chondrichthyes (e.g., sharks, rays) have internal fertilization regardless of whether they are egg-laying or live-bearing. In teleosts internal fertilization is rare; it necessarily occurs in the few live-bearers but also in some egg-laying species. In most live-bearers insemination takes place before ovulation. They copulate by an enlarged urogenital papilla or by a transformed anal fin. Sometimes only the female genital papilla is enlarged and can invade the male's vas deferens.

Eggs of all other teleosts are released before fertilization. Males and females swim close together so that the eggs are shed into a cloud of spermatozoa. Mating and courtship occur in many species, ensuring an intimate mixing of eggs and sperm.

CONTROL OF SPAWNING

Ripening of the eggs and spawning are controlled by hormones, by external factors, and by nutrition of the female. The pituitary gonadtropins trigger the ripening of the eggs and have an effect on spawning by controlling both gametogenesis and stereoidogenesis. Extirpation of the pituitary in teleosts leads to suppression of vitellogenesis; small oocytes don't grow, and developing oocytes which are already larger become atretic. The gonadal endocrine tissues fail to produce steroids. Similar suppression can be achieved by chemical treatment. The dual effect of the pituitary means that its hormones act both at the early gonadal development and during the period prior to spawning. The latter effect 'is often used in fish farming, e.g., in the culture of carps and in the production of caviar in sturgeons where spawning is induced by implantation or injection of pituitary tissue of the same or other species at a late stage of egg development.

While in nearly ripe fish a single dose is often enough to initiate spawning, repeated injections combined with changes in temperature and light periodicity may be required when the fish are rather unripe. The dependence of spawning on moon cycles in grunion (*Leuresthes tenuis*) spawning on California beaches is an extreme example of external factors controlling reproduction in fish.

Little is known about the mechanism by which temperature controls maturation and spawning. For many marine and freshwater fish the temperature range in which spawning occurs is rather narrow--in higher latitudes the minimum temperature tolerated for spawning is often the limiting factor for geographical distribution and for the successful introduction of a species into a new habitat. Data on minimum temperatures have to be established through rearing experiments under optimum conditions of salinity and oxygen. They may be much lower than the normal spawning temperature of the fish. In the Arcto-Norwegian tribe of cod which spawns in Vestfjorden between Lofotem Islands and the Norwegian mainland the fish stay in warm Atlantic water for some time and immigrate into a moderately warm intermediate layer of 4-7°C just for spawning. The eggs rise into cooler surface water of 2-4°C. Similar observations were made for the Atlanto-Scandian herring which overwinters in rather cold water east of Iceland and crosses the Norwegian Sea in the warm Norwegian current along the front of warm and cold water until it reaches the Norwegian coast. There it stays in the cold Baltic current for several days to weeks. Finally spawning takes place in warmer waters at about 6°C. All groups of summer-autumn spawning North Sea herring spawn at 12°C, the month and place of spawning varying from group to group according to the local temperature cycle.

The role of photoperiod in the maturation is not yet well understood. In herring it can't be very strong, as considerable shifts in spawning season from January to March have been observed in Atlanto-Scandian herring within recent decades (Devold 1963).

The rate of gonad growth is about the same in different groups of North Sea herring. The differences in spawning season of the populations are coordinated with differences in onset of gonad growth and in duration of a resting period just prior to spawning (Iles 1964). In Arctic cod photoperiod influences the thyroid gland and, through this, migratory activity which is linked with gonadal development. Cushing (1969) showed that in some fish stocks of temperate waters, e.g., plaice in the English Channel, the spawning season is more strictly fixed than one would expect if seasonal changes in temperature, vertical mixing, and food supply were the only timing factors. According to intensive sampling in 7 years between 1911 and 1950, plaice in the Southern Bight of the North Sea have a peak spawning date of 19 January with a standard error of 2.5 days. This suggests a time trigger of fair precision, e.g., seasonal changes in day length. However, female plaice spawn repeatedly at intervals of 1 to 2 weeks, thereby extending the spawning season over several weeks.

Within a population maturation and spawning time might differ. Long duration of the spawning season of a population might be due to prolonged spawning of the individual fish. But it may also be caused by differences in spawning time between age groups--older fish tend to spawn earlier in the season. Furthermore, the co-existence of different spawning groups must be taken into account. In the western Baltic

31

herring spawning takes place over several months in spring and again for a short period in autumn. Spring and autumn spawners are more or less distinct stocks, although some specimens may shift from one seasonal spawning pattern to the other, particularly at the limits of their distribution, as in the Baltic where herring of low relative fecundity tend to spawn in spring, regardless of whether the fish originated from spring or autumn spawning (Anokhina 1971).

In general, it is rather difficult to produce fully ripe eggs and sperm in captivity. In most cases, particularly when using small aquaria, oogenesis and/or spermatogenesis come to a halt at some intermediate stage. One example of successful artificial breeding is in the California anchovy, where continued production of eggs under laboratory conditions was brought about by keeping the fish under constant temperature conditions of 15°C and a light periodicity of less than 5 hours light per day (Leong 1971). More studies in the combined effect of cyclic changes of temperature and light on the reproduction cycle of marine fish are needed as a prerequisite of continuous aquaculture.

Feeding condition of the mother can have an important effect on the final maturation of the oocytes. In White Sea herring spawning may occur only every other year if environmental conditions, particularly food supply, are poor. Flüchter and Trommsdorf (1974) found no spawning in soles when they were fed with mussels over the whole maturation period. Injection of pituitary tissue did not induce spawning. Application of casein by forced feeding with cottage cheese brought the fish to spawn. Biochemical analysis of the mussels showed shortage of particular amino acids which are normally found in high quantities in the egg. The ovary draws them from the maternal tissues at a late stage of development. This puts the mother in a state of malnutrition, if the supply through food is insufficient. Indeed, Flüchter's soles showed signs of serious malnutrition--the blind side was blueish-red, and the normal white color returned only after treatment with casein.

IMPREGNATION AND FERTILIZATION

The first step of meiosis results in the class II oocytes. The second step brings about the haploid ovum; it takes place normally after ovulation and may be delayed even until after spawning and after the intrusion of the sperm into the ovum.

So far little is known about gamones for activation and attraction of the sperm in marine fish. Activity of sperm depends on the presence of small concentrations of Ca or Mg ions. In freshwater fertilization may be possible only at the very moment of sperm release into water, as salmonid sperm is active for less than a minute, and in sturgeon for only a few minutes. In seawater sperm is active for much longer periods. The fertilization rate of sperm of British Columbia herring was highest when eggs and sperm were kept separate for about 1 hour (14 °/oo salinity at 4°C) before mixing them (Alderdice and Velsen, personal communication). Sperm concentrations on two sites of British Columbia herring grounds averaged 150 per ml. Little is known about optimum concentration of sperm for successful fertilization; normally concentrations used in rearing experiments are manyfold higher than those quoted above (Hourston and Rosenthal 1976). The chorion of the egg is permeable for spermatozoa only through a small funnel, the micropyle, at the animal pole. Normally only one sperm is permitted to enter. The micropyle is closed afterwards. Polyspermy was found in some elasmobranchs, where one sperm fuses with the egg's nucleus, the rest being resorbed.

The sperm entering the egg has two functions: activation of the egg and fusion with the egg's nucleus. Activation leading to cleavage takes place normally after fertilization. The formation of the perivitelline space by intake of water through the pores of the chorion and afterwards the hardening of the chorion are important for the protection of the embryo at the early, most vulnerable stages. It is mainly the inner layer which hardens. The process is related to the alveolar colloids attached to the chorion and to hardening enzymes.

Data on fertilization rate in natural habitats are difficult to obtain. Only the absence of a perivitelline space can be taken as indicator of failure of fertilization. On the other hand, perivitelline spaces or cleavages may also occur without fertilization, due to various kinds of physical or chemical stimuli, e.g., in herring (Blaxter and Hempel 1961).

In general, it can be assumed that the fertilization rate under natural conditions is high; lower rates under experimental conditions are due to insufficient maturation or poor storage of gametes, and to lack of acclimation. In demersal eggs the fertilization rate may be somewhat lower if insemination occurs only after the eggs have settled, possibly some of them on their micropyle.

STORAGE OF GAMETES

For physiological experiments and for the purpose of selective breeding in aquaculture, the continuous availability of uniform gamete material is important. Eggs of freshwater fish can be kept in Ringer solution for some hours; eggs of herring, preferably the whole ovary, can be stored dry at about $4^{o}C$ for up to one week. Deep freezing of eggs proved not feasible because of their high water content. Sperm can be kept for many months by ultra-deep freezing, in liquid CO_2 (Blaxter 1955, herring sperm; Pullin 1972, plaice sperm) or in liquid N_2 (Mounib et al. 1968, cod sperm). In order to avoid destruction of the sperm by ice crystals the sperm has to be mixed with glycerol in diluted seawater or with ethylene glycol and lactose (Hoyle and Idler 1968, salmonids). The mixture is brought into close contact with liquid CO_2 ($-79^{o}C$) for quick freezing and can be transferred afterwards into liquid nitrogen ($-196^{o}C$) or kept in containers with solid CO_2. Blaxter (1955) achieved 80-85% fertilization rate in herring sperm stored for 6 months in solid CO_2. In liquid nitrogen, storage time should be almost unlimited. For thawing, the tubes with frozen sperm were transferred into a water bath of $40^{o}C$ before fertilization. The storage of sperm over long periods permits cross breeding of races spawning at different seasons or in areas which are far apart. This has been done in herring by Blaxter and Hempel (1961) by crossing Baltic and Norwegian spring spawners and crossing Baltic spring spawners and Buchan autumn spawners, and by Rosenthal (personal communication) who fertilized British Columbia herring eggs with sperm of Baltic herring after 1 year's storage of the sperm.

DEMERSAL AND PELAGIC EGGS

Almost all eggs of freshwater fish are attached to the substratum or

33

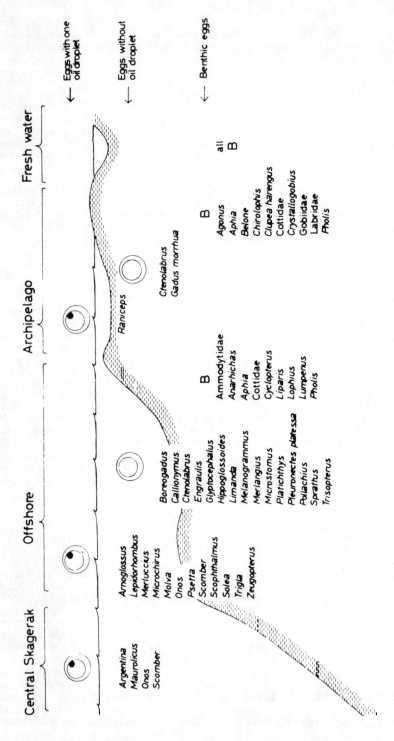

Fig. 19. The distribution of different types of eggs in the various zones of the Skagerak (Lindquist 1970).

34

float loosely on the bottom. This is not surprising if one considers that protein (the main substance in fish eggs) has a considerably higher specific gravity than freshwater. In rivers and brooks firm attachment to stones or plants or burial in gravel is essential to prevent downstream drift.

Demersal eggs in marine fish might be phylogenetically an old character, considering that fish originated in freshwater. Indeed, among the marine groups which spawn demersally ancient groups such as osmerids and clupeoids predominate. However, demersal spawning must have developed independently in several groups, as there are many other fish of the littoral and upper sublittoral zones which have demersal eggs. On the Arctic and Antarctic shelf fish eggs are mainly demersal, with large yolk reserves and long incubation periods. Examples are Greenland cod (*Gadys ogac*), Arctic flounder (*Pseudopleuronectes americanus*), sea wolf (*Anarhichas lupus*) and Antarctic nototheniids. Demersal spawning protects the eggs against the low salinity of the surface water during the melting of the ice and against the risk of freezing. In some marine fish, such as capelin, the eggs drift loosely on the sea bed; in others, like herring, they are sticky for a very short period after spawning or they have hairy filaments or curled strings to fix them to the substratum (*Belone* and *Scyliorhinus*, respectively).

Lindquist (1970) described the general distribution of pelagic eggs with and without oil globules and of demersal eggs in the Skagerak, which is characterized by a dome-shaped central gyre with an outflow of Baltic water and an inflow of North Sea water. In the shallow coastal waters the majority of species produce demersal eggs. The central "oceanic" waters of the Skagerak are occupied by pelagic eggs with oil droplets. In the offshore neritic zone pelagic eggs without oil droplets predominate (Fig. 19). In other areas the same zonation may be spread over a much wider distance.

Demersal spawners are often rather particular regarding the selection of substratum. Herring spawning in a tank with different kinds of sediments no longer extruded any eggs when passing from the favorite gravel to the fine sediments. In Barkley Sound Pacific herring selected seaweed as the spawning substratum. Divers observed similar selectivity in capelin. Preference for gravel is also found in the spawning beds of salmon, presumably as a protective measure against silting of the eggs.

The development of egg patches of herring in the Firth of Clyde was described by Baxter (1971). The females extrude a narrow ribbon of eggs while swimming close to the bottom; the male fish swimming above the females release milt into the water. The mass spawning extends over days and weeks with new groups of fish entering the spawning area while the spent fish leave. In the course of the spawning season the egg patch increases in its extent. Patches of eggs in an advanced stage of development seem to be avoided by spawning herring, but new eggs may be deposited on top of layers which are only a few days old.

PARENTAL CARE AND LIVE-BEARING

This is a subject which has attracted much attention by ethologists and ecologists and is described in much detail in various textbooks and popular publications. Only a few comments on marine fish will be made here. There is a line of increasing parental care from deposition of eggs on a selected substratum to complete protection of egg masses inside the mother or the father. The eggs of capelin are partly buried in the sediment. The male lumpsucker protects the egg mass against fish, starfish, and crabs, and blows water over them almost continuously for several weeks. Sticklebacks build nests of twigs and leaves, and gobiids lay their eggs in the shell of a bivalve.

The next stage of care is the protection by the parent body. The most primitive form is the gunnel (*Pholis*) which rolls its egg mass into a ball and then one of the parents coils around the eggs. More advanced is the care in the brood pouch of male sea horses and pipe fishes. In various catfishes, eggs are carried at the ventral part of the body or at the forehead. Mouth brooding either by the male or the female is found in several freshwater families but also in some marine catfishes. Live-bearing fish, i.e., species with internal fertilization and internal incubation of the embryos, are common in Chondrichthyes, but in teleosts they are restricted to eight families of Cyprinodontiformes and Perciformes. Embryogenesis can take place within the follicle, e.g., prior to ovulation or--more common--in the ovarian cavity after ovulation. Live-bearing can be viviparous sensu stricto if the embryo develops in close contact with the nourishing maternal tissue. No egg membrane covers the embryo. In the case of ovoviviparity, which is far more common even in Chondrichthyes, the mother may or may not nourish the embryo which stays in the ovary (teleosts) or Mullerian duct (skates and rays), but embryo and maternal tissue are separated by the egg membrane. The embryo may hatch within the ovary and remain there for some time before parturition.

The different degrees of dependence from the mother can be estimated from the change in dry weight of the egg from fertilization until parturition. In some truly viviparous Poecilidae the dry weight increases rapidly. Those eggs contain little yolk and take their nourishment from the mother. In other families the dry weight of yolk plus embryo remains more or less constant, the mother covering the expenses for basic metabolism. In *Sebastes* the egg loses weight--an indication for little or no contribution of the mother to the eggs after fertilization.

In the commercially important *Sebastes marinus* the annual reproductive cycle was studied by Magnusson (1955). In males the gonads reach their maximum size in summer but mating takes place in October to January. At that time the urinary bladder is swollen, its wall is folded and is a strong muscle. It shows much excretory activity. At the time of mating the eggs are not ripe and the female has to store the sperm until March when fertilization takes place, presumably after the eggs have left the follicles. Within a female all embryos are the same size. The larvae hatch inside the mother and are born soon afterward in May-June, i.e., 2 to 3 months after fertilization and 6 to 7 months after mating. At that stage their oxygen demand presumably exceeds the supply provided by the mother, although in this group of species a special vascular system to the ovary ensures a particularly good gas exchange (Moser 1967). In some species of Cottidae spawning of the eggs occurs only a few days after fertilization.

SUMMARY

Factors controlling the ripening of eggs and the onset of spawning include hormones, feeding condition of the mother, and external stimuli, particularly temperature and light. In marine teleost fish external fertilization after extrusion of the eggs is the rule, internal fertilization and live-bearing being the exception. This is in contrast to Chondrichthyes and partly also to freshwater fish.

The period of activity of spermatozoa is very long in seawater compared with freshwater where sperm is active only for a few seconds to minutes. Artificial fertilization in marine fish is rather simple due to the longevity of the sperm, provided fully ripe males and females are available. However, in captivity, most marine fish do not produce ripe eggs or sperm, at least not under the conditions usually provided in public aquaria and laboratory tanks. Artificial cross-breeding between different spawning groups is facilitated by easy storage and transport of sperm. While sperm can be stored ultradeep frozen in glycerine with solid CO_2 or liquid nitrogen, no method is known to keep eggs alive for fertilization for longer than a week after death of the mother. As a rule marine fish eggs are pelagic and freshwater fish eggs are demersal. However, demersal eggs are fairly common in many marine families, mainly ancient groups and those of coastal distribution. Parental care and live-bearing are also more often found in nearshore fishes than in oceanic species.

PHYSIOLOGY AND ECOLOGY OF EGG STAGES

The morphogenesis during the incubation period, i.e., from fertilization until the larva leaves the eggshell, is fully described in various textbooks of zoology and comparative embryology. Blaxter (1969) gave a summary of the major events. Only a few morphological facts about early development after fertilization should be mentioned here. Major emphasis of the chapter is on the physiological aspects of survival and normal development of eggs as related to environmental factors.

EMBRYONIC DEVELOPMENT STAGES

At fertilization the yolk is already partly concentrated at the vegetative pole (teleolecithal eggs). After fertilization the cytoplasm concentrates quickly in the region of the animal pole. Elasmobranchs and teleosts perform meroblastic cleavages which lead to the formation of a blastodermal cap. As cleavage is not complete, the deeper layers of the periblast form an acellular layer surrounding the yolk. Nuclei immigrate into the periblastic syncytium which is responsible for mobilizing the yolk. During the first few cleavages the cells are still able to compensate for the loss of some cells. At the early stages of development the yolk has obviously regulatory functions in embryogenesis; at later stages it serves as the nutrient basis only. The embryonic shield of a minnow (*Fundulus*) has been encultured after complete removal of the yolk.

At the next stage, proliferating peripheral cells of the blastoderm progressively form a coat over the yolk (epiboly), until the last uncovered area, the so-called blastopore, is closed. At that time the embryo becomes visible as a rod which soon develops the outlines of eyes and auditory sacs. When the embryo is about half-way around the yolk, the heart starts beating and the first traces of pigmentation appear at the embryo's dorsal parts. The primordial fin becomes visible as a dorsal fold. The embryo becomes raised from the yolk and the tail

38

becomes freely movable. In the final stage before hatching the embryo usually surrounds the yolk by a little more than one full circle. In fish with a long incubation period the eyes are fully pigmented and there are often characteristic patterns of black and yellow/greenish pigmentation on the embryo's body.

For a fishery biologist it is of interest to know the age of an egg, i.e., the time passed after spawning. The major embryonic development from the first cleavages to the formation of a primitive embryo takes place during the first few days or less after fertilization in most pelagic eggs. The later longer part of the incubation period is for growth and differentiation of the embryo. Therefore, the time passed after spawning can be determined in young stages by the state of embryonic development and in older stages by the length of the embryo. Although embryonic development is a continuous process, Apstein (1909) divided the incubation period into 25 "stages." For most purposes in fishery biology a rough scale of five stages is sufficient and can be used for any kind of teleost egg.

Stage   I.   Fertilization - Gastrulation (blastopore closed)
Stage   II.   Embryo surrounds the yolk up to 180°
Stage   III. Embryo surrounds the yolk up to 270°
Stage   IV.   Embryo surrounds the yolk up to 360°
Stage   V.   Embryo surrounds the yolk by more than 360°

Often the stage I is divided into stage Ia and Ib, in separating gastrula formation from the earlier stages.

Figures 20 and 21 show the developmental stages as given by Apstein (1909) for plaice and a series of photographs of developing eggs of cod.

DURATION OF INCUBATION IN RELATION TO TEMPERATURE

The incubation period differs greatly from species to species. The larvae of some species hatch at a very early embryonic stage (anchovy, salmonids), others are far more developed (herring) (Fig. 22). At their normal temperature range incubation lasts, e.g., for 2-4 days in sardines, 2-3 weeks in plaice, 5 months in salmon, and 2 years in piked dogfish.

Temperature, oxygen tension, and, to a lesser extent, salinity influence the rate of development and determine the date of hatching. In Atlanto-Scandian herring spawning at 5^oC, it takes 25-29 days for the eggs to hatch, and in North Sea herring 9-12 days at its normal spawning temperature of 12^oC (Fig. 23). When incubated at the intermediate temperature of 8^oC, the large larvae of Atlanto-Scandian herring tend to hatch about the same day as the much smaller North Sea larvae. Genetic differences between herring races are small in the rate of embryonic development and in the stage at which larvae leave the eggshell. However, hatching rate at 12^oC was better in North Sea herring than in Norwegian herring which are adjusted to lower temperatures.

In order to allow for the influence of temperature on incubation (Fig. 24), it was again Apstein (1909) who introduced the term "Tagesgrade" (day degrees) when he found in plaice that the product of number of degrees centigrade above "biological zero" and the time to reach a given developmental stage were nearly constant. On the basis of

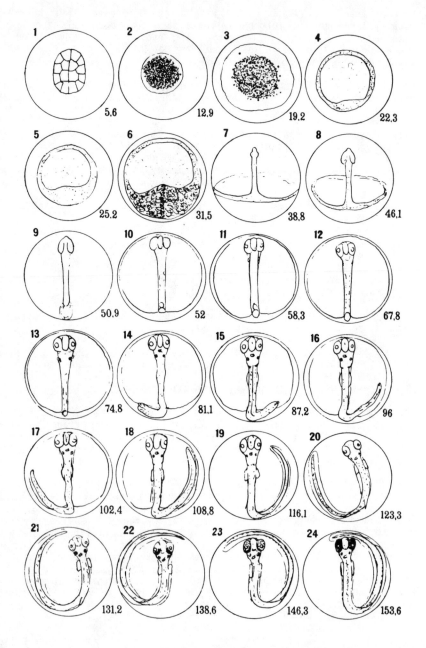

Fig. 20. Egg development of plaice (*Pleuronectes platessa*
L.) (Apstein 1909), and day degrees required to reach
the various stages indicated by the numbers on the
figure.

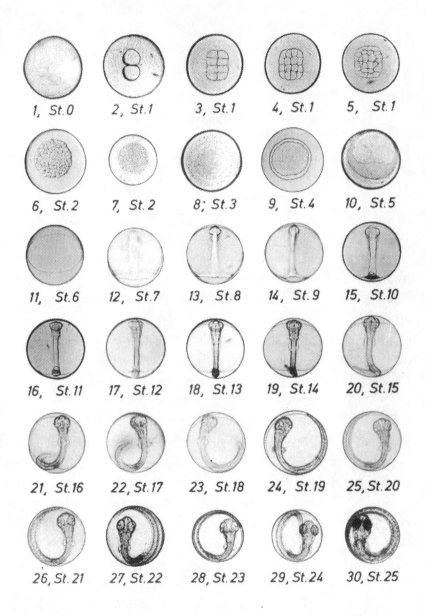

Fig. 21. Stages of development of eggs of cod (*Gadus morhua*) (photograph Pommeranz and Kuhnhold).

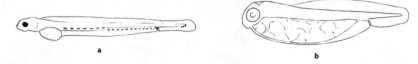

Fig. 22. Newly hatched larvae of (a) herring (*Clupea harengus*) and (b) northern anchovy (*Engraulis encrasicholus*).

experiments he produced a table showing for each of the 25 developmental stages the duration in days at 1-centigrade intervals for cod, dab, plaice, and flounder eggs. The extrapolated origin of the day-degrees line, erroneously called "biological zero," is normally below 0°C, in plaice at -2.4°C, in herring (depending on the race) -1.3° to 0°C. The egg stops development at higher temperatures depending on its temperature tolerance limit which in turn is higher under given adverse salinity and oxygen conditions. In fact the time-temperature relationship is an exponential function and the "Tagesgrade" concept of a linear relationship is only valid for a narrow range of temperatures, normally encountered by the eggs in their habitat. At very low temperatures the number of day-degrees is higher, and at high temperatures it is lower than normally found in the given species.

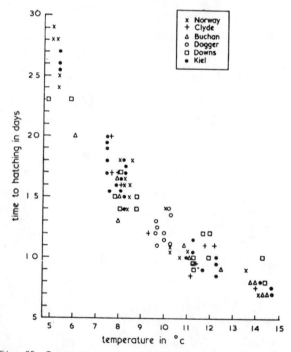

Fig. 23. Temperature dependence of incubation time in herring of different origins (Blaxter and Hempel 1963).

Riley (1974) demonstrated that the effect of temperature on rate of development is about the same for the entire incubation period, i.e., the ratio between the developmental stages I-IV is not affected by temperature (Fig. 25). However, at high temperatures larvae hatch at a premature developmental stage but with a small yolk sac.

Several attempts were made to formulate the temperature-time relationship for incubation in a more satisfactory way (Blaxter 1969). However, for most practical purposes the day-degrees calculated on the basis of a "biological zero" are quite sufficient.

There is only a rough relationship between egg size and number of day-degrees until hatching of the larva, as shown below:

Species	Day-degrees	Egg size (mm)
Flounder (*Platichthys flesus*)	56	0.8 - 1.1
Dab (*Limanda limanda*)	59	0.6 - 1.0
Herring (*Clupea harengus*)	140	0.9 - 1.7
Cod (*Gadus morhua*)	150	1.1 - 1.6
Plaice (*Pleuronectes platessa*)	165	1.7 - 2.2
Salmon (*Salmo salar*)	400	5.0 - 6.0

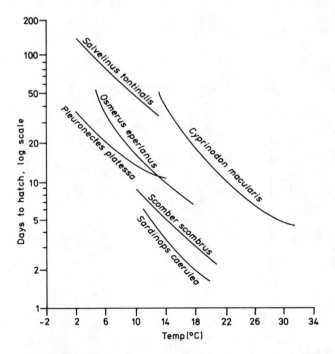

Fig. 24. Incubation time at different temperatures in various species of marine and freshwater fish (various authors, after Blaxter 1969).

In general, lowering of salinity results in a prolongation of incubation period in marine fish. Lack of oxygen retards the rate of embryonic development and causes premature hatching. The combined effects of the environmental factors on development are discussed in the following paragraphs.

OXYGEN CONSUMPTION

The oxygen uptake in eggs increases rapidly in the course of development. A salmon egg at fertilization has an O_2-uptake of 0.2 µl/hr but at hatching of 3.4 µl/hr (Hayes et al. 1951). In herring the corresponding figures are 0.01 µl/hr and 0.07 µl/hr. The increase in O_2-consumption with age in herring eggs (Braum 1973) is not a continuous, smooth curve. There is a rapid rise during the first 4 days until the ectodermal folding; from there the curve flattens until the heart beats and contractions of the rump muscles start and such activity causes additional O_2-consumption. During the last days before hatching O_2-consumption may level off because of difficulties in O_2-supply through the shell.

Total oxygen consumption in the eggs of southern pigfish, *Congiopodus leucopaecilus*, over the 14 days incubation period increases from 2 µl/egg/day (at the second day) to 8 µl/egg/day (at hatching) (Robertson 1974). In Pacific sardines O_2-consumption per mg dry weight and hour doubles from 0.5 µl O_2 at 20 hours after

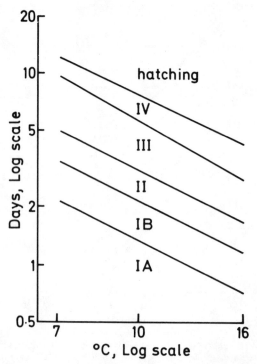

Fig. 25. Incubation times to the end of the various developmental stages in sole eggs (after Riley 1974).

44

fertilization to ca 1 µl O_2 at hatching about 60 hours later. This refers to oxygen consumption of non-moving embryos (standard consumption). As soon as the embryo starts movements in the eggshell the oxygen consumption (active consumption) increases by the factor 2-3 (Hayes et al. 1951, Lasker 1962).

Standard consumption is of course temperature-dependent. In herring eggs reared at 8°C standard O_2-consumption amounted to 1.5 µl/mg/hr and at 12°C to 4 µl/mg/hr.

General estimates of metabolism and of efficiency of embryonic growth can be made by combining data on oxygen consumption with those on decrease in yolk weight and increase in somatic weight of the embryo. The conversion of yolk matter into embryonic tissue and the combustion of yolk in metabolism will not be dealt with in this book. The utilization of yolk as studied, e.g., in herring (Blaxter and Hempel 1963; Paffenhöfer and Rosenthal 1968), in sole (Flüchter and Pandian 1968), and in southern pigfish (Robertson 1972), is a continuous process starting at ovulation (i.e., at the end of incorporation of yolk matter into the egg and ending at the end of the yolk sac stage of the larva).

The oxygen demand of the early embryo is partly covered by the oxygen stores in the yolk and particularly in the perivitelline fluid. Therefore, anoxic external conditions will not inhibit early development until gastrulation. From thereon anoxia results often in the accumulation of lactic acid and in retardation of development and/or in lack of heart beat or movements of the embryo. Those effects of anoxia are reversible if short-term. Apart from internal regulatory mechanisms which compensate for external oxygen deficiencies for short periods, there is a permanent uptake of oxygen from the surrounding water, ovarial fluid, or maternal tissues. In marine fishes with pelagic eggs O_2-uptake does not pose serious problems to the egg because of the oxygen saturation in the sea and the high permeability of the chorion.

OSMOREGULATION AND BUOYANCY

Inside the chorion the vitelline membrane covers yolk and cytoplasm. Chorion is a direct product of the ovary, while the vitelline membrane is produced by the egg itself. After activation of the egg by fertilization or by external effects the vitelline membrane detaches itself from the chorion. The perivitelline space develops between both membranes. The primary egg membrane had produced colloidal substances rich in polysaccharides which, due to their high osmotic pressure, draw water from outside the chorion until an osmotic equilibrium is reached between the perivitelline water and the surrounding water. Therefore with a given amount of osmotic active substances in the perivitelline space, its volume and hence egg diameter are larger in low salinity water than in full seawater, e.g., the eggs of North Sea sprat have only a very narrow perivitelline space, but a large one in Baltic sprat eggs. The embryo can be protected against osmotic changes by the vitelline membrane which is either impermeable or osmoregulatory-active. In other cases, e.g., herring, osmoregulation is done by the ectodermal cells covering the embryo and its yolk after gastrulation. The first type is typical for fish with pelagic eggs. It ensures constant specific gravity and osmotic pressure in eggs from directly after fertilization. Ectodermal osmoregulation, as found in herring, starts late, and the embryonic body fluid tends to be isosmotic for some time after fertilization. These eggs cannot float (Hohendorf 1968).

The buoyancy of marine fish eggs is mainly the result of the high amount of water of low salinity in the embryo and yolk. In certain species the oil globules play an additional role in achieving buoyancy. It should be stressed that the perivitelline water does not contribute to the buoyancy of the egg.

The water in cytoplasm and yolk (combined, called ovoplasm) originates from the ovarial fluid which depends only to a small extent on the habitat salinity. North Sea flounders transferred to salinity conditions of the central Baltic (6.5 ^{o}/oo) for 3 weeks prior to spawning still spawn eggs which are buoyant at 20 ^{o}/oo salinity. Similarly, Baltic flounders kept for 2 years in water of full marine salinity (35 ^{o}/oo) still produced eggs of low specific gravity (Solemdal 1973). At full marine salinity pelagic eggs have well balanced buoyancy which keep the eggs in midwater. Problems in buoyancy arise when sea fish invade brackish water habitats, e.g., the occupation of the Baltic by marine fish (Hempel and Nellen 1974). There the difference in density between embryonic water and the habitat water becomes very small--the uplift by the embryonic water might be insufficient to keep the egg floating; this limit is reached in Baltic cod, flounder, and turbot at 10-12 ^{o}/oo salinity, in sprat at 6.5 ^{o}/oo. There are actually only very few species with pelagic eggs which have established populations under low salinity conditions. Their eggs are characterized by impermeability of the vitelline membrane, low salinity of the ovarial and embryonic fluid, and high water content of the embryo, leading to a considerable increase in egg size. While dry weight of Baltic cod eggs is 40% less than in the North Sea, the egg volume is larger by 10%. A particular adaptation to low salinity is found in some populations of flounder (*Platichthys flesus*) and turbot (*S. rhombus*) in the central Baltic. Their eggs do not float but develop on the sea bed. In those populations egg size is the same as in the North Sea.

The thickness of the chorion is an important factor in regulating specific gravity of fish eggs, as the chorion is of particularly high density and amounts to up to one-third of the total dry weight. Pelagic eggs in the Baltic have much thinner egg shells than in the North Sea. It is only in the special case of demersal eggs of eastern Baltic flounder that the chorion is thick; these differences are genetically fixed (Lonning and Solemdal 1972).

TEMPERATURE TOLERANCE

Temperature tolerance of eggs may be described for a freshwater fish, yellow perch (Hokanson and Kleiner 1974). Similar features were found in marine fish. Survival of the eggs and hatching of viable larvae are the two important criteria of tolerance.

Eggs were fertilized at their optimum temperature of 12°C (fertilization rate 95%) and were immediately afterwards transferred into test temperatures. There was no hatching above 25°C and below 3°C. Up to 5°C the few hatching larvae were not viable. More than 70% viable larvae were observed only at the small range of 13°-16°C, although a good hatching rate was found at the wider range between 9°-18°C. In a second set of experiments fertilized eggs remained at the optimum temperature until the neural keel formed. Only afterwards eggs were transferred into test temperatures. The main difference between the results of the first and the second experiments was in the improved production of viable larvae at high temperatures. In general, tolerance limits for the early embryonic stages were 3°-20°C, for older embryonic stages 7°-23°C (Fig. 26).

The increase in tolerance during incubation time was also described by Irvin (1974) in eggs of Dover sole (*Solea solea*). While incubation was successful between 12° and 22°C, optimum yields of swim-up larvae were reached with temperatures rising from 5°C as initial incubation

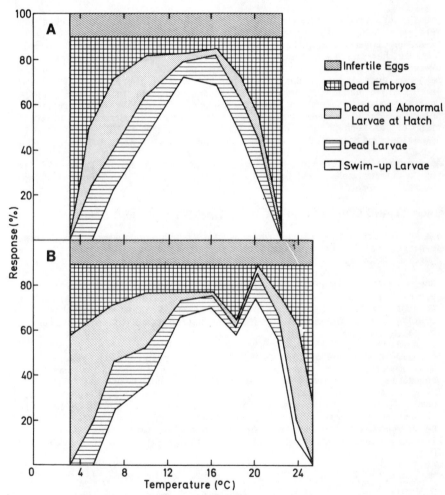

Fig. 26. Effect of temperature on fertilization rate, hatching rate and viability of larvae in yellow perch (*Perca flavescens*): a) constant test temperature from fertilization to swim-up stage; b) incubation at 12°C until neural keel formed; afterwards until swim-up stage various test temperatures (Hokanson and Kleiner 1974).

temperature to 10°C at a rate of 0.5°-1°C/day. A temperature rise--although at a lower rate--is frequently met under natural early summer conditions. This favors shorter hatching periods and lower incidences of abnormalities at hatching. Below 7°C the hatched larvae were smaller and less developed. Above 16°C larval size decreased again with increasing temperature.

In some species fluctuating temperatures yield better hatching rates than constant temperatures; this is predictably the case in shallow water fish which are subjected to those changes due to tidal effects and diurnal warming of the water. Acclimation of the mother influences the tolerance of the eggs (Hubbs and Bryan 1974).

The temperature tolerance of eggs is smaller than that of larvae and very much smaller than that of adult fish. In eggs of temperate water fish the range between the upper and lower lethal temperatures is only 14°C in herring (with racial differences in the actual limits), and 6°-10°C in eggs of fish spawning in the open sea. The narrow tolerance range of eggs is still sufficient for survival in the marine environment but it might become important with aquaculture and in the vicinity of cooling water outlets of coastal power plants. The difference in tolerance range between eggs, larvae (plus some juveniles), and adult fish of different latitudes is shown by Brett (1972). Figure 27 summarizes literature data of about 50 species.

Adults have a tolerance range of up to 22°C in tropical fish, 20°C in the temperate zone, and around 8°C in coldwater fish of Arctic and Antarctic stenotherm species.

SALINITY AND COMBINED EFFECTS OF TEMPERATURE AND SALINITY

Due to the protection of the inner medium of the egg against the outside seawater, tolerance of changes in salinity is very good in most marine eggs. Eggs of fully marine species like plaice and cod can be reared at 5-6 °/oo salinity, although the fertilization rate is somewhat lowered under conditions abnormal to the given species or race. In several species the range of salinity tolerance is smaller before gastrulation and just before hatching than in the middle of the incubation period. As mentioned above, in marine fish incubation tends to be prolonged at low salinities.

In cod, plaice, and flounder von Westernhagen (1970) studied the combined effects of temperature and salinity on hatching rate and occurrence of abnormalities, particularly bending of the tail and inflation of the yolk sac (at low salinities). In cod best survival was found at the combinations 4°C : 25 °/oo and 6-8°C : 30 °/oo. In flounder the optimum range was much wider (2°-8°C : 25 °/oo - 33 °/oo). The optimum temperature was higher at higher salinities in cod and flounder. In plaice the optimum combination was around 6°C : 20 °/oo (Fig. 28).

Salinity optima and tolerance for embryonic development are much lower in brackish water populations, e.g., in coastal herring (Dushkina 1973). Even within the Baltic in which salinity decreases from west to east, different populations with different optima have themselves established. In view of the short geological history of the Baltic this can be taken as an indication of the high selective value of adaptations related to reproduction.

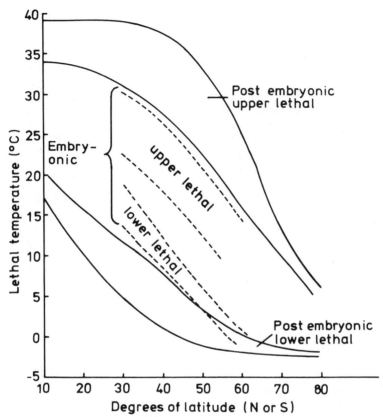

TOLERANCE

Fig. 27. General distribution of upper and lower lethal
temperatures for eggs and for larvae and juveniles of
fish of different geographical latitudes (after Brett
1972).

Similar studies in haddock (*Melanogrammus aeglefinus*) off Iceland (von
Westernhagen 1968) demonstrated the narrow salinity range for normal
embryonic development at low temperatures: no survival at 0.3°-0.6°C at
any salinity, normal hatching only above 30 °/oo at 2°C. Salinity tolerance increased at 4°-6°C, where hatching occurred even at 17 °/oo. At
8°C the development was again disturbed, with no hatching at 30 °/oo and
reduced hatching rates even in full seawater. The distribution of
spawning places of haddock around Iceland agrees well with their temperature optimum. The spawning places are limited by the 4°C and 7°C
isotherm. On the other hand, the temperature/salinity relationship of
haddock eggs explains why this species fails to reproduce successfully
in the western Baltic. There the early spring temperatures are too low
for haddock to tolerate low salinities.

The effects of temperature/salinity on the various stages of development
in the flatfish (*Parophrys vetulus*) was demonstrated by Alderdice and

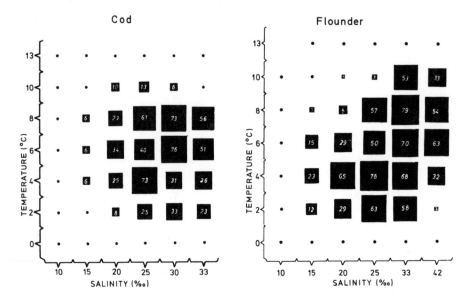

Fig. 28. Percentage survival from fertilization until commencement of feeding stage of larvae in cod and flounder of the western Baltic at different combinations of constant temperature and salinity. The size of the black squares is proportional to the percentage survival (Source: von Westernhagen 1970).

Forrester (1968). Their results are summarized in Fig. 29. For different measures of response optimum salinity varies: maximum larval length is achieved at 28 °/oo, while maximum total hatch and maximum viable hatch were found at 25-26 °/oo, viability of larvae being favored by slightly lower temperatures than total hatching rate.

The authors described mathematically the interaction of temperature and salinity and of acclimation on development and metabolism. The method is based on the calculation of response surfaces. One of the merits of those models is to minimize the number of combinations in experiments to predict the combined effects of two or more environmental factors. Alderdice (1972) gave a review of the methods for studying combinations of environmental effects.

This method has been applied in one of the most intensive studies of the joint effects of temperature and salinity on the development of a marine fish which was carried out by Fonds et al. (1974) using the garfish *Belone belone*. The authors measured several attributes of early development, various measures of body size at hatching, and subsequent survival at neural stage, hatching, and as larvae. In all those attributes the effect of temperature was much higher than of salinity (e.g., number of vertebrae, Fig. 30). The optimum temperature/salinity relationship for the egg stage is found at slightly higher salinity and lower temperature than the optimum temperature/salinity relationship for larval size and survival.

50

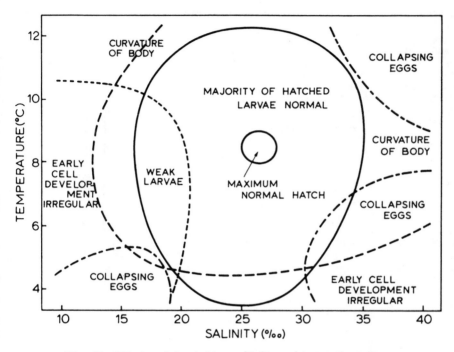

Fig. 29. Effects of incubation salinity and temperature on viability of developing eggs of the flatfish (*Parophrys vetulus*) (Alderdice and Forrester 1968).

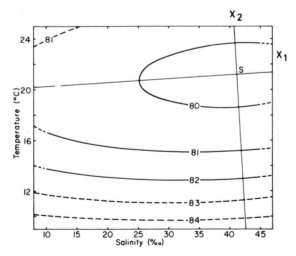

Fig. 30. Isopleth digram showing predicted changes in mean number of vertebrae of larval garfish incubated at different temperature/salinity combinations (modified from Fonds et al. 1974).

OXYGEN AND OTHER GASES AS LIMITING FACTORS

In most habitats of marine fish eggs oxygen is not a limiting factor. Pelagic eggs drift near the surface in water of high oxygen content. Exceptions to this rule are in the central Baltic and other stratified brackish-water habitats where we find the so-called brackish-water submergence. Eggs of Baltic cod occur at 80-100 m, i.e., at much greater depth than normally encountered. Due to their specific buoyancy the eggs remain below the thermocline. Those deep layers show a periodic oxygen deficiency.

Lack of oxygen is also met by pelagic fish eggs in upwelling areas where water of the intermediate oxygen minimum layer appears near surface. Oxygen is further depleted by the high biological activity in those areas.

Demersal eggs are far more frequently confronted with reduced levels of dissolved oxygen. The literature on salmonid eggs incubated at low oxygen tensions was summarized by Blaxter (1969). The development is generally retarded and the larvae hatch at a smaller size. Tolerance for low O_2-tension increases immediately after hatching. That shows the barrier effect of the chorion. Survival in herring eggs decreased only at less than 25% O_2-saturation. The highest sensitivity is found after about one-third of the incubation period. In general, however, the tolerance limit rises with stage of development and is even higher at non-optimal temperature and salinity conditions.

Detailed studies on herring eggs (Braum 1973) showed different critical levels of O_2 demand at the various stages of development. At optimum temperature and salinity, herring eggs showed abnormal embryogenesis if exposed to low oxygen concentrations. No hatching was observed at less than 20% O_2-saturation, the degree of abnormalities being related to the O_2 values. If the reduction of O_2-tension took place only after blastoderm formation, normal embryonic discs developed. In that case the initial intake of O_2-saturated water at the formation of the perivitelline space created an oxygen reservoir for normal development. However, even in this case metabolism was reduced and larvae hatched at a smaller length than normal. At 100% saturation larvae hatched at about 8 mm length; at 20% saturation larvae measured only 6-7 mm.

At the sea bed water exchange by near bottom currents is of primary importance for the oxygen supply for the demersal eggs, as diffusion is not sufficient to ensure sufficient levels of O_2 in the egg. Experimentally Braum (1973) found 50% mortality in herring eggs at current velocities of 0.03 cm/sec. He expects velocities of this order and below in thick layers of herring eggs. Taylor (1971) found in experiments with *Clupea pallasi* a correlation between egg mass thickness and mortality which doubled already at about five layers. Under most experimental conditions mortality in herring eggs tends to be higher even at lower egg concentration than in nature.

In coastal spawning of Pacific herring, eggs are more often deposited in seaweed and eelgrass than on rocks and gravel. Females seem to select the plants and lay the eggs in a manner which ensures free circulation of water through the egg mass. Studies in spawning beds of Atlantic herring rarely showed considerable density-dependent mortality in carpets which were up to eight egg layers thick (Baxter 1971). Only in very thick lumps of herring eggs as sometimes encountered at the

Norwegian coast and in the North Sea (Runnstrom 1941; Hempel and Schubert 1969) was the frequency of dead eggs in the inner layers high. It is very possible that high concentrations of metabolites may have adverse effects on development and survival in addition to the effects of oxygen deficiencies.

Little is known about the effect of other gases on fish eggs and larvae. Increased CO_2 reduces O_2 uptake of eggs in freshwater, possibly through reducing pH, but seawater is well buffered against changes in pH in contrast to freshwater. Occurrence of free hydrogen sulfide is also rare in seawater except in sites with very high BOD's due to hypertrophication, high organic sedimentation, or active dumping of particulate sewage. H_2S is highly toxic to eggs and young larvae, far more than to older stages (Smith and Oseid 1974). It disturbs or inhibits spawning, delays the hatching, and reduces hatching rate drastically. In fish with long incubation periods size of larvae at hatching was much more reduced by H_2S than in fish with short incubation periods.

LIGHT AND OTHER RADIATION

The demersal eggs of salmonids which are normally deposited in gravel are particularly sensitive to visible light. In rainbow trout the sensitivity increases until the heartbeat starts, later dropping drastically. High illumination results in early hatching of small larvae. Hamdorf (1960) found evidence for the destruction of lactoflavin in trout eggs by visible light. Lactoflavin plays a crucial role in the production of respiration enzymes and through them its lack may cause a complete failure or a restriction of the respiration. This explains both retardation in development and early hatching. Blue light has the greatest, and yellow and orange light the smallest, deleterious effects. Eggs which are red by carotinoids or bright yellow by high concentration of lactoflavin are far more resistant against light than eggs with little pigmentation.

The demersal eggs of herring seem also somewhat sensitive to light. Blaxter (1956) found higher hatching rates in eggs kept in darkness. It seems worthwhile to look into possible racial differences in this respect in view of the great variety of spawning habitats ranging from the littoral zone to deep water. Pelagic eggs are often highly resistant against visible light (e.g., sole, angler fish) although they are normally not protected by pigmentation.

Breder (1962) discussed the importance of transparency of eggs and larvae for their survival. Transparency is typical for marine pelagic eggs which occur in brightly illuminated places. Those larvae hatch at an early stage of development. Transparency is considered as a protection, particularly against heat radiation which will pass through the transparent egg and early larva with little absorption. However, pigmentation at the embryo's or larva's integument will protect the more sensitive tissues by absorbing the light. The role of transparency as a protective measure against predation is considered by Breder as of secondary importance in view of the fact that many planktophages may not depend on visual feeding. Heavily pigmented eggs are common in certain groups of fish which occur mostly in shaded locations. They are demersal and have a long incubation period.

Eggs exposed to ultraviolet radiation revealed reduced hatching rates in various marine species (Marinaro and Bernard 1966). In studying the risks for plaice eggs to life near the sea surface, Pommeranz (1974) found mortality not directly dependent upon the applied dose of total daylight but upon its ultraviolet component. Therefore, survival was much better when the daylight was filtered through ordinary glass plates. The threshold for mortality was between 250 and 460 ly/d. Plaice eggs in the North Sea encounter in January up to 50 ly/d, in February 100 ly/d, and in March 200 ly/d. This applies only to eggs which stay permanently in the uppermost 10 cm, as ultraviolet light does not penetrate deep into the water column.

Infrared light was only rarely tested. It was found dangerous to eggs of smelt and perch (Eisler 1961). X-rays have a strong effect on the first stages of development from fertilization to blastodisc stage; later on much higher doses are tolerated. Major effects vary from immediate death through deformities and, at larval stages, destruction of haematopoetic tissues and decrease in numbers of erythrocytes.

MECHANICAL FORCES

Two kinds of effects of mechanical damage of the eggs are possible: 1) Abnormalities and mortality caused by vibrations and shaking at the early stages of development. Fish farmers strictly avoid transport of newly fertilized eggs of salmonids, etc. Similar mortalities after mechanical disturbance at early incubation stages can be observed in marine eggs, such as those of herring, cod, and plaice. 2) Destruction of the chorion. In a number of experiments Pommeranz (1974) applied various kinds of forces to plaice eggs at different stages of development. He pressed the eggs and measured the force needed to deform them by a certain percentage. Deformation had to exceed 70% before the thin chorion burst and it was only the bursting of the chorion which led to mortality. Hardening of the chorion is a very quick process. During the first 10 hours after fertilization "crushing force" rose from 1.5 g to about 500 g and reached 700 g at the end of gastrulation. From there the crushing force decreased slowly and reached very low values at hatching.

At different developmental stages the same deformation is of different degrees of danger for the later viability of the larvae. Pommeranz summarized his findings as follows:

1) first 11 hours: very low resistance;
2) until embryo has surrounded half the yolk, mechanical resistance is high but viability of the embryo is low;
3) later embryonic stages: mechanical resistance and viability are high;
4) prior to hatching: low mechanical resistance but high viability.

From the very little we know about the forces occurring in rough weather at the sea surface we can assume that the egg is endangered by wave action during the very first hours only.

One hour's spray by a sprinkler caused little mortality in eggs kept in a shallow dish, but 24 hours' sprinkling killed the eggs. Air bubbles from an aerator had a slightly detrimental effect on the eggs during the third to sixth day. Those treatments were meant to simulate forces found in a wind-activated sea.

Fishermen have often expressed concern about the possible destruction of demersal egg-beds by the bobbins and otter boards of trawls. This question can hardly be answered by experimental shaking of herring eggs as attempted by Burd and Wallace (1971), who found diminished viability of larvae after shaking the eggs at certain stages of development. Far more conclusive were diving observations of the spawning beds of capelin (Bakke and Bjorke 1973). At a heavily fished spawning ground about 1% of the area was disturbed by trawl boards, the capelin eggs being pushed away. Experiments with large bobbins towed in front of divers resulted in no obvious destruction of eggs. Between 6-10% of the eggs which were whirled up from the bottom by the bobbins resulted in moribund larvae, while the untouched control produced 0-2% moribunds. The trawling experiment was carried out at a rather less sensitive intermediate stage of embryonic development (Dragesund et al. 1973). Disturbances at the onset of embryogenesis may have a more deleterious effect. However, even if all eggs which were whirled up by fishing at the spawning ground under inspection died, the total loss of eggs due to fishing operations would not exceed 1%. Nevertheless, the experiments also point to a so-far unknown cause of natural mortality, as eggs get whirled up in shallow waters by wave action and swift currents. Bakke and Bjorke (1973) assume that mainly in shallow areas 5-10% of the eggs were destroyed over the 4 weeks' incubation period at north Norwegian spawning grounds. Similar studies should be carried out with British Columbia herring eggs, of which a considerable number is also washed away in bad weather.

DISEASES AND PREDATION

No detailed study of diseases in fish eggs caught at sea has been reported. Seawater is generally poor in free bacteria and fungi except in inshore and estuarine areas and in most rearing tanks. On the other hand, the egg's surface seems to be an attractive substratum for microorganisms. Heavy coverage of the chorion by bacteria, fungi, and ciliates is therefore rather common in rearing experiments, particularly in closed circulation systems. The mucous microbial film on plaice eggs can lead to a sticking together of the eggs, to increased mortality, or to weakening of the embryos. Ultraviolet radiation of the water entering the incubator and treatment with antibiotics (e.g., Shelbourne 1974, used mixtures of streptomycin and penicillin in plaice) were frequently applied to reduce losses by diseases. In freshwater fish hatcheries dealing with fish of very extended incubation periods, microbial control is routine practice.

Much speculation is going on among fishery and marine biologists on predation of fish eggs. Demersal eggs of Atlantic herring and capelin are preyed upon by haddock, saithe, capelin, and others. The presence of "spawny" haddock (having herring spawn in their guts) has been used by fishermen to locate spawning grounds of herring. Although we may assume that the stomach contents of one "spawny" haddock or saithe contains at least an amount of eggs equal to the total seasonal production of one herring, no reliable assessments of predation are possible, as we do not know the digestion rate and hence the feeding frequency of haddock nor is the total number of fish concentrating on herring spawn known. The same holds for the predation by birds feeding on the littoral and upper sublittoral carpets of herring (*Clupea pallasi*) and capelin. Surprisingly little predation by invertebrates is reported for demersal fish eggs. Starfish seem to avoid egg carpets and no heavy concentrations of crab have been observed on herring beds.

Obviously pelagic eggs are much more subject to predation although, at first sight, it seems easier to feed on a carpet or lump of herring eggs than to pick single transparent eggs from the water column. There seem to be no predators specializing on ichthyoplankton. But it is the great number of nonspecialized plankton feeders of all systematic groups and size categories which cause high mortality by taking pelagic fish eggs together with other plankton organisms of suitable size. Pelagic fish eggs and larvae are found in plankton-feeding crustacea, in arrow worms (*Sagitta*) and in all kinds of plankton-feeding fish. In those predators ichthyoplankton mostly play a minor role in the entire diet, as they may be taken at about the same intensity as other plankton. Further, Kuhlmann (1977) showed that *Sagitta* prefer copepods to fish eggs, which they cannot detect. This also might be the case with other plankton feeders which respond only to vibrations or rapid movements as performed by planktonic Crustacea.

Ctenophores, particularly *Pleurobrachia*, have been accused by several authors as being one of the most important causes of egg mortality. Experimental studies by Greve (1972) demonstrated the large volume of water searched by *Pleurobrachia* per day. Therefore, mass mortality may occur if fish eggs happen to pass through a layer of *Pleurobrachia*. However, over a 4-year period in Scottish waters Fraser (1970) found that stomach contents of *Pleurobrachia* were very poor in ichthyoplankton. They did contain large amounts of crustacean and molluscan plankton of a size range appropriate for fish larval food, however. He concluded that *Pleurobrachia* is more a competitor than a predator to ichthyoplankton. Dinoflagellates of the genus *Noctiluca* feed voraciously on fish eggs. Hattori (1962) reported heavy predation on anchovy eggs which might even result in reduction in year class strength of anchovy larvae in years of high abundance of *Noctiluca*.

FIELD ESTIMATES OF EGG MORTALITY

Estimates of mortality in demersal egg beds are based on three different methods: a) grab sampling, b) direct observations and sampling by divers, and c) inspection of stomach contents of egg-eating fish (Hempel and Hempel 1971). Success of grab sampling is largely dependent on guidance by underwater television or divers' observations. Divers are operating mostly on the shallower spawning grounds and are often limited by poor visibility in inshore waters.

In general, mortality in the egg stage is very low in demersal marine eggs except during early developmental stages. For various spawning grounds of herring and of capelin figures are normally below 10%. Those figures do not include to predation by fish and birds and the mortality at hatching and immediately afterwards. Hatching mortality was studied by Galkina (1971) who transferred advanced eggs of *Clupea pallasi* from sublittoral spawning grounds to the laboratory and observed that eggs which were originally very densely packed on the spawning grounds had rather low hatching success. Many larvae were too weak to leave the egg shell or they died soon afterwards. This, however, is open to the criticism that transfer, etc., may have affected the eggs.

Estimates of mortality in pelagic eggs are also subject to considerable methodological difficulties. In contrast to demersal eggs, the pelagic eggs are not stationary but change their position by horizontal drift and vertical movements. On the other hand, pelagic eggs are more evenly distributed over a large area--particularly if incubation periods extend over more than a few days. Furthermore, they are easy to sample, with ordinary quantitative plankton gear. The most recent summary of problems and methods of fish egg surveys has been published by Smith and Richardson (1977). We will take work on North Sea plaice as an example for mortality estimates.

The simplest way to estimate mortality during the egg phase would be the estimate of abundance of eggs of different developmental stages in a plankton sample. This would only be reliable if spawning intensity were constant over a long period. However, as it normally fluctuates, it is necessary to follow a certain group of eggs during the incubation period; i.e., after a certain period which equals about 80% of the incubation time at the ambient temperature the survey has to be repeated and now the abundance of the latest stages has to be estimated. This normally involves a wider area allowing for the drift during the incubation period. The decrease in egg number from stage I during the first survey to stage V during the second survey reflects overall egg mortality. Far more detailed information can be obtained if sampling is carried out repeatedly at fixed intervals over the entire spawning season and if all stages of development are taken into account. This is a costly and time-consuming project and has been carried out with sufficient effort on only a few occasions.

The spawning grounds of plaice in the English Channel, Southern Bight, and central North Sea were sampled by surveys between 1962 and 1971. A large high-speed sampler was used to collect the pelagic stages of plaice together with the whole plankton community. Development rates of eggs and larvae in relation to water temperature were measured in laboratory experiments. The further treatment of samples and data is described by Bannister et al. (1974, p. 23) as follows:

"The counts of ten different categories of eggs and larvae at each station on each cruise were charted, contoured at selected levels and the total abundance in the cruise area was calculated by planimetry (*see* Simpson 1959). These values were then corrected for the stage duration, using the temperatures observed at sea, in order to estimate numbers produced per day for each development stage on each cruise. Annual production curves for each development stage in each season were then plotted, using the mid-point of the cruise as the mean sampling date. The final estimates of seasonal production for each stage were made by measuring the areas under these curves. The values determined in this way were used to estimate the losses between stages in each season.

By using the mean sea temperature for production period, the average duration for each stage was calculated. By plotting seasonal abundance against cumulative stage duration (age) generalized loss-rate curves were obtained for each season. The instantaneous coefficient of loss per day, Z, can then be derived from these seasonal data either as $N_2/N_1 = e^{-Zt}$ (where N_1 is the initial number of eggs or larvae and N_2 the number surviving to the next stage in the period t days, t being the mean stage duration), or from fitted regressions of $\log_e$ numbers of eggs or larvae produced in each stage, against their cumulative stage durations (Harding and Talbot 1970)."

Average differences in abundance of stage I and stage V eggs amount to

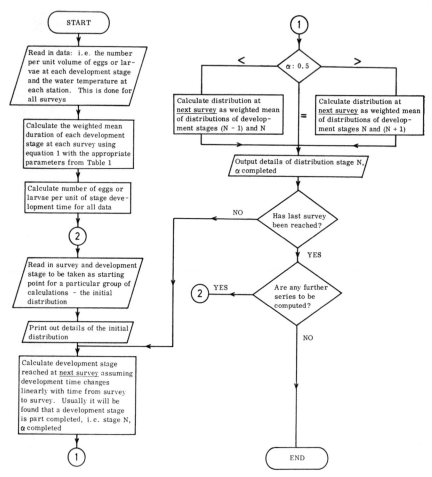

Fig. 31. Flow chart of first stage processing results of repeated ichthyoplankton surveys in the study of changes in distribution (Talbot 1977).

egg mortalities of 70-83% in plaice eggs of the southern North Sea and Irish Sea. This is higher than the figures of 50% mortality assumed by Buchanan-Wollaston (1926) and Simpson (1959). Harding et al. (1978) compared the results of 11 years of plaice egg and larva surveys in the Southern Bight of the North Sea. Total egg mortality fluctuated between 53% and 85% with average Z-values between 0.04 and 0.14. The mortality figures for the individual developmental stages are highly variable, partly because of sampling errors. The causes for the year-to-year differences in plaice egg mortality are still unknown.

In cod of the southern North Sea and in sole of British inshore waters very high egg mortalities were recorded (94%, 95.6%-99.9%, respectively, Harding et al. 1974). During the incubation period of California sardines lasting 4 days, the daily instantaneous mortality rate was $Z = 0.3$, and the overall egg mortality is at least 75%, not including late mortality at the hatching stage (Smith 1973). Southward and Demir (1974) observed an overall mortality of 54% in pilchard eggs of the English Channel. In the laboratory mortality of pelagic eggs can be kept at a much lower level of 5-10%.

The dispersal of eggs plays a major role in the estimates of mortality in eggs with a long incubation period such as those of North Sea plaice. Talbot (1977) combined measurements in the distributions of plaice eggs and larvae with dye tracer Rhodamine B-experiments and an array of moored current meters. The ichthyoplankton surveys were carried out over the entire season and repeated for several years. Figure 31 shows how data sets of ichthyoplankton distribution can be processed after the survey has been concluded and the plankton material has been sorted. From the results of the calculations sets of distributions can be deduced. Each set starts from a particular cruise and developmental stage and shows the resultant distribution at the time of subsequent cruises. Figure 32 gives an example for the results of the 1962 survey, depicting, over 8 weeks, the fate of the eggs which were at stage Ia at the first of seven subsequent cruises. It can be seen that the spread of the eggs changed surprisingly little over the incubation period, turbulent diffusion being at a comparatively low rate. Vertical shear diffusion played a much greater role in an area of strong tidal flows. Residual currents, varying from year to year, transport the ichthyoplankton patches along the axis of the Southern Bight of the North Sea.

SUMMARY

The incubation period can be divided into a short period of initial embryogenesis and a longer time span of growth of the embryo. The early

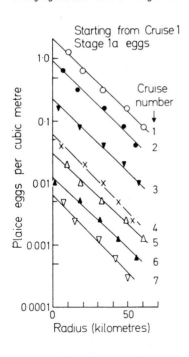

Fig. 32. Dispersal of an individual group of plaice eggs and larvae in the southern North Sea during 7 subsequent cruises covering the period January 23 to April 1, 1962 (Talbot 1977).

morphogenesis in the egg is characterized by meroblastic cleavages leading to the blastoderm cap. By epiboly the periblastic syncytium covers the yolk. The embryo develops as a rod, pressing itself into the yolk's surface. The embryo grows quickly in length. The differentiation of the primordial fin develops while the embryo's tail gets lifted from the yolk.

The effect of temperature on incubation time can be expressed in day-degrees over a range of medium temperatures. Low O_2 tension retards embryonic development but forces premature hatching. Mortality and abnormal development occur only at rather high O_2 deficiency.

The temperature tolerance of eggs is less than the tolerance of the larvae and adult fish. The temperature range in which a high percentage of viable "swim-up" larvae hatch is much narrower than the overall temperature tolerance and is influenced both by salinity and by O_2 tension.

In general, marine fish eggs are rather resistant to changes in ambient salinity. Nevertheless, much experimental effort has been put into the analysis of the effects of salinity and temperature/salinity combinations on marine fish eggs in spite of the fact that salinity is rather stable in the sea except in nearshore waters and brackish areas.

In demersal eggs, washing away and bird predation of nearshore deposits are considered serious mortality factors; deeper deposits are often heavily preyed upon by various fish species.

There is little evidence that pelagic fish eggs become damaged by a wave action except during the first few hours after fertilization, although the embryo can suffer from mechanical stress during early stages of development. Nevertheless, egg mortality in pelagic eggs is much higher than in demersal eggs, due to the great number of plankton feeders. Until hatching, the number of specimens is reduced by an order of magnitude. The main cause of this mortality is presumably predation by plankton feeders.

Has the wide dispersion of offspring so many advantages that they outnumber the risks of life as a small plankton organism? Pelagic eggs are mostly single. Does the scatter of the eggs reduce predation or is it just a further step toward wide distribution? The question remains to be answered.

REFERENCES

Ahlstrom, E. H. 1965. A review of the effects of the environment of the Pacific sardine. ICNAF Spec. Publ. 6:53-74.

Alderdice, D. F. 1972. Factor combinations. Responses of marine poikilotherms to environmental factors acting in concert. Pages 1695-1722 *in* O. Kinne, ed. Mar. Ecol. 1(3).

Alderdice, D. F., and G. R. Forrester. 1968. Some effects of salinity and temperature on early development and survival of the English sole (*Parophrys vetulus*). J. Fish. Res. Board Can. 25:495-521.

Anokhina, L. E. 1960. Relationship between the fertility, fat content and the variations in the size of ova in the clupeid fishes. Tr. Soveshch. Ikhtiolog. Komis. Akad. Nauk SSSR 13:290-295 (in Russian).

Anokhina, L. E. 1963. Some aspects of the fecundity of the herring in the White Sea. Rapp. P.-V. Réun. ICES 154:123-127.

Anokhina, L. E. 1971. Maturation of Baltic and White Sea herring with special reference to variations in fecundity and egg diameter. Rapp. P.-V. Réun. ICES 160:12-17.

Apstein, C. 1909. Die Bestimmung des Alters pelagisch lebender Fischeier. Mitt. d. deitsch. Fischereivereins 25:364-373.

Bagenal, T. B. 1963. Variations in plaice fecundity in the Clyde area. J. Mar. Biol. Assoc. U.K. 43:391-399.

Bagenal, T. B. 1966. The ecological and geographical aspects of the fecundity of the plaice. J. Mar. Biol. Assoc. U.K. 46:161-186.

Bagenal, T. B. 1969. The relationship between food supply and fecundity in brown trout *Salmo trutta* L. J. Fish. Biol. 1:167-182.

Bagenal, T. B. 1971. The interrelation of the size of fish eggs, the date of spawning and the production cycle. (Marine and fresh-water.) J. Fish. Biol. 3:207-219.

Bagenal, T. B. 1973. Fish fecundity and its relations with stock and recruitment. Rapp. P.-V. Réun. ICES 164:186-198.

Bakke, S., and H. Bjørke. 1973. Diving observations on Barents Sea capelin at the spawning grounds off northern Norway. Fiskeridir. Skr. Havundersøk. 16:140-147.

Bannister, R. C. A., D. Harding, and S. J. Lockwood. 1974. Larval mortality and subsequent year-class strength in the plaice (*Pleuronectes platessa* L.). Pages 21-37 *in* J. H. S. Blaxter, ed. The early life history of fish. Springer, Heidelberg.

Baxter, I. B. 1971. Development rates and mortalities in Clyde herring eggs. Rapp. P.-V. Réun. ICES 160:27-29.

Blaxter, J. H. S. 1955. Herring rearing I. The storage of herring gametes. Mar. Res. 3:1-12.

Blaxter, J. H. S. 1956. Herring rearing II. The effect of temperature and other factors on development. Mar. Res. 5:1-19.

Blaxter, J. H. S. 1968. Rearing herring larvae to metamorphosis and beyond. J. Mar. Biol. Assoc. U.K. 48:17-28.

Blaxter, J. H. S. 1969. Development: Eggs and larvae. Pages 177-252 *in* W. S. Hoar and D. J. Randall, eds. Fish physiology III. Acad. Press, New York.

Blaxter, J. H. S., and G. Hempel. 1961. Biologische Beobachtungen bei der Aufzucht von Heringsbrut (Engl. summary). Helgolander Wiss. Meeresunters. 7:260-283.

Blaxter, J. H. S. and G. Hempel. 1963. The influence of egg size on herring larvae (*Clupea harengus* L.). ICES 28:211-240.

Blaxter, J. H. S., and G. Hempel. 1966. Utilization of yolk by herring larvae. J. Mar. Biol. Assoc. U.K. 46:219-234.

Blaxter, J. H. S., and F. G. T. Holliday. 1963. The behaviour and physiology of herring and other clupeoids. Pages 261-393 *in* F. S. Russell, ed. Adv. Mar. Biol. Vol. 1.

Botros, G. A. 1962. Die Fruchtbarkeit des Dorsches (*Gadus morhua* L.) in der westlichen Ostsee und den westnorwegischen Gewassern. Kieler Meeresforgh. 18:67-80.

Braum, E. 1973. Einflusse chronischen exogenen Sauerstoffmangels auf die Embryogenese des Herings (*Clupea harengus*) Neth. J. Sea Res. 7:363-375.

Breder, C. M. 1962. On the significance of transparency in osteichthid
fish eggs and larvae. Copeia 1962:561-567.

Brett, J. R. 1972. Temperature: fishes. Pages 515-560 *in* O. Kinne,
ed. Mar. Ecol. Vol. 1.

Bruce, J. R. 1924. Changes in the chemical composition of the tissues
of the herring in relation to age and maturity. Biochem. J.
18:469-485.

Buchanan-Wollaston, H. J. 1926. Plaice-egg production in 1920-21,
treated as a statistical problem, with comparison between the data
from 1911, 1914, and 1921. Fish. Invest. Ser. II, 9(2).

Bückmann, A. 1950. Die Untersuchungen der Biologischen Anstalt (Helgoland) uber die Okologie der Heringsbrut in der sudlichen Nordsee.
I. Helgolander wiss. Meeresunters. 3:1-57.

Burd, A. C., and P. D. Wallace. 1971. The survival of herring larvae.
Rapp. P.-V. Réun. ICES 160:46-49.

Bussmann, B. 1978. Untersuchungen hitzestabiler Peptide in den Eiern
des Ostsee-Herings (*Clupea harengus* L.). Meeresforsch. 26:96-108.

Cushing, D. H. 1957. The number of pilchards in the Channel. Fish.
Invest. Lond. 21(5). 27 pp.

Cushing, D. H. 1969. The regularity of the spawning season in some
fishes. J. Cons., ICES 33:81-92.

Cushing, D. H. 1973. Recruitment and parent stock in fishes. Univ.
Washington, Washington Sea Grant Publ. 73-1. 97 pp.

Devold, F. 1963. The life history of the Atlanto-Scandian herring.
Rapp. P.-V. Réun ICES 154:98-108.

Dragesund, O. 1970. Factors influencing yearclass strength of
Norwegian spring spawning herring (*Clupea harengus* L.).
Fiskeridir. Skr. Havundersøk. 15(4):381-450.

Dragesund, O., J. Gjøsaeter, and T. Monstad. 1973. Estimates of stock
size and reproduction of the Barents Sea capelin in 1970-1972.
Fiskeridir. Skr. Havundersøk. 16:105-139.

Dushkina, L. A. 1973. Influence of salinity on eggs, sperm and larvae
of low-vertebral herring reproducing in the coastal waters of the
Soviet Union. Internat. J. on life in oceans and coastal waters.
Mar. Biol. 19:210-223.

Ehlebracht, J. 1973. Stoffliche Veranderungen wahrend des Reifezyclus
in Ovarien von Herbst- und Fruhjahrsheringen der westlichen Ostsee.
Ber. dt. wiss. Kommn. Meeresforsch. 23:47-83.

Ehrenbaum, E. 1905-1909. Eier und Larven von Fischen. Nordisches
Plankton 1. 413 pp.

Eisler, R. 1961. Effects of visible radiation on salmonid embryos and
larvae. Growth 25:281-346.

Fagetti, E. 1973. Selected bibliography on identification of pelagic marine fish eggs and larvae. Pages 59-82 *in* G. Hempel, ed. Fish eggs and larval surveys. (Contributions to a manual.) FAO Fish. Tech. Pap. No. 122.

Flüchter, J., and T. J. Pandian. 1968. Rate and efficiency of yolk utilization in developing eggs of the sole *Solea solea*. Helgolander Wiss. Meeresunters. 18:53-60.

Flüchter, J., and H. Trommsdorf. 1974. Nutritive stimulation of common sole (*Solea solea* L.). Ber. dt. wiss. Kommn. Meeresforsch. 23:352-359.

Fonds, M., H. Rosenthal, and D. F. Alderdice. 1974. Influence of temperature and salinity on embryonic development, larval growth and number of vertebrae of the garfish, *Belone belone*. Pages 509-525 *in* J. H. S. Blaxter, ed. The early life history of fish. Springer, Heidelberg.

Fraser, J. H. 1970. The ecology of the ctenophore *Pleurobrachia pileus* in Scottish waters. J. Cons., ICES 33:149-168.

Fulton, T. W. 1891. The comparative fecundity of sea fishes. Rep. Fish. Board Scotl. 9:243-268.

Galkina, L. A. 1971. Survival of spawn of the Pacific herring (*Clupea pallasii* Val.) related to the abundance of the spawning stock. Rapp. P.-V. Réun. ICES 160:30-33.

Gotting, K. J. 1961. Beitrage zur Kenntnis der Grundlagen der Fortpflanzung und zur Fruchtbarkeitsbestimmung bei marinen Teleosteern. Helgolander Wiss. Meeresunters. 8:1-61.

Greve, W. 1972. Økologische Untersuchungen an *Pleurobrachia pileus*. 2. Laboratoriumsuntersuchungen. Helgolander Wiss. Meeresunters. 23:141-164.

Hamdorf, K. 1960. Die Beeinflussung der Embryonal- und Larvalentwicklung der Regenbogenforelle (*Salmo irideus* Gibb.) durch Strahlung im sichtbaren Bereich. Z. vergl. Physiol. 42:525-565.

Harden Jones, F. R. 1968. Fish migration. Arnold, London.

Harder, W. 1964. Anatomie der Fische I and II. Handbuch der Binnenfischerei Mitteleuropas, Schweizerbarth, Stuttgart.

Harding, D., and J. W. Talbot. 1973. Recent studies on the eggs and larvae of plaice (*Pleuronectes platessa* L.) in the Southern Bight. Rapp. P.-V. Réun. ICES 164:261-269.

Harding, D., J. H. Nichols, and J. D. Riley. 1974. Preliminary estimates of egg production and mortality in the 1968 North Sea cod spawning. ICES CM 1974/F:21 (mimeo).

Harding, D., J. H. Nichols, and D. S. Tungaty. 1978. The spawning of plaice (*Pleuronectes platessa* L.) in the southern North Sea and the English Channel. Rapp. P.-V. Réun. ICES 172:102-113.

Hattori, S. 1962. Predatory activity of Noctiluca on anchovy eggs. Bull. Tokay Reg. Fish. Res. Lab. 9:211-220.

Hayes, F. R., D. Pelluet, and E. Gorham. 1953. Some effects of temperature on the embryonic development of the salmon (*Salmo salar*). Canad. J. Zool. D31:42-51.

Hempel, G., ed. 1973. Fish egg and larvae surveys. (Contributions to a manual.) FAO Fish. Tech. Pap. No. 122. 82 pp.

Hempel, G. 1974. Summing up of the symposium on the early life history of fish. Pages 757-759 *in* J. H. S. Blaxter, ed. The early life history of fish. Springer, Heidelberg.

Hempel, G., and J. H. S. Blaxter. 1967. Egg weight in Atlantic herring (*Clupea harengus* L.). J. Cons., ICES 31:170-195.

Hempel, G., and W. Nellen. 1974. Fische der Ostsee. Pages 215-232 *in* G. Rheinheimer, ed. Meereskundee der Ostsee. Springer, Heidelberg.

Hempel, G., and K. Schubert. 1969. Sterblichkeitsbestimmungen an einem Eiballen des Nordseeherings. Ber. dt. wiss. Kommn. Meeresforsch. 20:79-83.

Hempel, I., and G. Hempel. 1971. An estimate of mortality in eggs of North Sea herring (*Clupea harengus* L.). Rapp. P.-V. Réun. ICES 160:24-26.

Hensen, V. 1895. Ergebnisse der Plankton-Expedition der Humboldt Stiftung. Methodik der Untersuchungen. 1:1-200. Kiel und Leipzig.

Hensen, V., and C. Apstein. 1897. Die Nordsee-Expedition 1895 des Deutschen Seefischereivereins. Uber die Eimenge der im Winter laichenden Fische. Wiss. Meeresunters. Helgoland 2(2). 101 pp.

Hilge, V. 1975. Geschlechtsreifung und Laichreifung bei Teleosteern. Ber. dt. wiss. Kommn. Meeresforsch. 24:172-183.

Hilge, V. 1977. On the determination of the stages of gonad ripeness in female bony fishes. Ber. dt. wiss. Kommn. Meeresforsch. 25:149-155.

Hjort, J. 1914. Fluctuations in the great fisheries of northern Europe viewed in the light of biological research. Rapp. P.-V. Réun. ICES 20:1-228.

Hoar, W. S., and D. J. Randall, eds. 1969. Fish physiology. Vol. 3. New York, Acad. Press. 483 pp.

Hohendorf, K. 1968. ZurSchwebfahigkeit pelagischer Fischeier in der Ostsee. Vorlaufige Mitteilung. Ber. dt. wiss. Kommn. Meeresforsch. 19:181-193.

Hokanson, K. E. F., and Ch. F. Kleiner. 1974. Effects of constant and rising temperatures on survival and developmental rates of embryonic and larval yellow perch, *Perca flavescens* (Mitchill).

Pages 437-448 *in* J. H. S. Blaxter, ed. The early life history of fish. Springer, Heidelberg.

Holliday, F. G. T., J. H. S. Blaxter, and R. Lasker. 1964. Oxygen uptake of developing eggs and larvae of the herring (*Clupea harengus*). J. Mar. Biol. Assoc. U.K. 44:711-723.

Hourston, A. S., and H. Rosenthal. 1976. Sperm density during active spawning of Pacific herring (*Clupea harengus pallasii*). J. Fish. Res. Board Can. 33:1788-1790.

Hoyle, R. J., and D. R. Idler. 1968. Preliminary results in the fertilization of eggs with frozen sperm of Atlantic salmon (*Salmo salar*). J. Fish. Res. Board Can. 25:1295-1297.

Hubbs, C., and C. Bryan. 1974. Effect of parental temperature experience on thermal tolerance of eggs of *Menidia audens*. Pages 431-435 *in* J. H. S. Blaxter, ed. The early life history of fish. Springer, Heidelberg.

Iles, T. D. 1964. The duration of maturation stages in herring. J. Cons. ICES 29:166-188.

Irvin, D. N. 1974. Temperature tolerance of early developmental stages of Dover sole, *Solea solea* (L.). Pages 449-463 *in* J. H. S. Blaxter, ed. The early life history of fish. Springer, Heidelberg.

Kandler, R., and W. Pirwitz. 1957. Uber die Fruchtbarkeit der Plattfische im Nordsee-Ostsee-Raum. Kieler Meeresforsch. 13:11-34.

Kinne, O. 1977. Cultivation: Fishes. Pages 968-1035 *in* O. Kinne, ed. Mar. Ecol. 3(2). Chichester, John Wiley.

Kuhlmann, D. 1977. Laboratory studies on the feeding behaviour of the chaetognaths *Sagitta setosa* J. Muller and *S. elegans* Verril with special reference to fish eggs and larvae as food organisms. Ber. dt. wiss. Meeresforsch. 25:163-171.

Kupffer, C. 1878. Die Entwicklung des Herings aus dem Ei. Wiss. Meeresunters. Abt. Kiel 3:175-226.

Lagler, K. F., J. E. Bardach, and R. R. Miller. 1962. Ichthyology. John Wiley, New York. 545 pp.

Lasker, R., and G. H. Theilacker. 1962. Oxygen consumption and osmoregulation by single Pacific sardine eggs and larvae (*Sardinops caerulea* Gerard). J. Cons., ICES 27:25-33.

Leong, R. 1971. Induced spawning of the northern anchovy, *Engraulis mordax* Girard. NOAA Fish. Bull. 69:357-360.

Lindquist, A. 1970. Zur Verbreitung der Fischeier und Fischlarven im Skagerak in den Monaten Mai und Juni. Inst. Mar. Res. Lysekil Ser. Biol. Rep. No. 19:1-82.

Lönning, S., and P. Solemdal. 1972. The relation between thickness of chorion and specific gravity of eggs from Norwegian and Baltic flatfish populations. Fiskeridir. Skr. Havundersøk. 16:77-87.

Magnusson, J. 1955. Mikroskopisch-anatomische Untersuchungen zur
Fortpflanzungsbiologie des Rotbarsches (*Sebastes marinus* L.). Z.
Zellforsch. 43:121-167.

Marinaro, J. Y., and M. Bernard. 1966. Contribution a l'etude des
oeufs et larves pelagiques de poissons mediterraneens. 1. Note
preliminaire sur l'influence lethale du rayonnement solaire sur les
oeufs. Pelagos 6:49-55.

May, R. C. 1971. An annotated bibliography of attempts to rear the
larvae of marine fishes in the laboratory. NOAA Tech. Rep.,
NMFS SSRF 632. 24 pp.

May, R. C. 1974. Larval mortality in marine fishes and the critical
period concept. Pages 3-20 *in* J. H. S. Blaxter, ed. The early
life history of fish. Springer, Heidelberg.

Mengi, T. 1963. Veranderungen in der chemischen Zusammensetzung des
reifenden Ovariums des Ostseedorsches. Kieler Meeresforsch.
21:107-121.

Meyer, H. A. 1878. Biologische Beobachtungen bei kunstlicher Aufzucht
des Herings der westlichen Ostsee. Wiegandt, Hempel und Parey,
Berlin.

Milroy, Th. 1908. Changes in the chemical composition of the herring
during the reproductive period. Biochem. J. 3:366-390.

Moser, H. G. 1967. Seasonal histological changes in the gonads of
Sebastes paucispinis Ayers, an ovoviviparous fish (Family
Scorpaenidae). J. Morphol. 123:329-353.

Mounib, M. S., P. C. Hwang, and D. R. Idler. 1968. Cryogenic
preservation of Atlantic cod (*Gadus morhua*) sperm. J. Fish. Res.
Board Can. 25:2623-2632.

Nikolski, G. V. 1969. Theory of fish population dynamics. Oliver and
Boyd, Edinburgh. 323 pp.

Oosthuizen, E., and N. Daan. 1974. Egg fecundity and maturity of
North Sea cod, *Gadus morhua*. Netherl. J. Sea Res. 8:378-397.

Paffenhofer, G. A., and H. Rosenthal. 1968. Trockengewicht und Kalo-
riengehalt sich entwickelnder Heringseier. Helgolander wiss.
Meeresunters. 18:45-52.

Parrish, B. B., and A. Saville. 1965. The biology of the north-east
Atlantic herring populations. Oceanogr. Mar. Biol. Annu. Rev.
3:323-373.

Peters, H. M. 1963. Eizahl, Eigewicht und Gelegeentwicklung in der
Gattung *Tilapia* (Cichlidae, Teleostei). Int. Rev. Hydrobiol.
48:547-576.

Polder, J. J. W. 1961. Cyclical changes in testis and ovary related
to maturity stages in North Sea herring, *Clupea harengus* L. Arch.

Nierl. Zool. 14:45-60.

Pommeranz, T. 1974. Resistance of plaice eggs to mechanical stress and light. Pages 397-416 *in* J. H. S. Blaxter, ed. The early life history of fish. Springer, Heidelberg.

Pullin, R. S. V. 1972. The storage of plaice (*Pleuronectes platessa*) sperm at low temperatures. Aquaculture 1:279-283.

Raitt, D. S. 1933. The fecundity of the haddock. Fish. Board Scotl. Sci. Invest. 1:1-42.

Riley, J. D. 1974. The distribution amd mortality of sole eggs (*Solea solea* L.) in inshore areas. Pages 39-52 *in* J. H. S. Blaxter, ed. The early life history of fish. Springer, Heidelberg.

Robertson, D. A. 1974. Developmental energetics of the southern pigfish (Teleostei: Congiopodidae). N.Z.J. Mar. Freshw. Res. 8:611-620.

Rollefsen, G. 1962. Fisken og den gater. Norsk fiskeriforskning fram til i dag. Pages 30-55 *in* G. Rollefsen, ed. Havet og vare Fisker. Eides Forlag, Bergen. Vol. 1.

Royce, W. F. 1972. Introduction to the fishery sciences. Acad. Press. New York, London. 351 pp.

Runnstrom, S. 1941. Quantitative investigations on herring spawning and its early fluctuations on the west coast of Norway. Fiskerdir. Skr. Havundersøk 6. 71 pp.

Russell, F. S. 1926. The vertical distribution of marine macroplankton III. Diurnal observations on the pelagic young of teleostean fishes in the Plymouth area. J. Mar. Biol. Assoc. U.K. 14:387-414.

Russell, F. S. 1976. The eggs and planktonic stages of British marine fishes. London, Acad. Press. 524 pp.

Schopka, S. A. 1971. Vergleichende Untersuchungen zur Fortpflanzungsrate bei Herings- und Kabeljaupopulationen (*Clupea harengus* L. und *Gadus morhua* L.). Ber. dt. wiss. Kommn. Meeresforsch. 22:31-79.

Schopka, S. A., and G. Hempel. 1973. The spawning potential of populations of herring (*Clupea harengus* L.) and cod (*Gadus morhua* L.) in relation to the rate of exploitation. Rapp. P.-V. Réun. ICES 164:178-185.

Scott, D. P. 1962. Effect of food quantity on fecundity of rainbow trout (*Salmo gairdneri*). J. Fish. Res. Board Can. 19:715-731.

Sette, O. E. 1943. Biology of the Atlantic mackerel (*Scomber scombrus*) in North America. Part I. U.S. Fish Wildl. Serv., Fish. Bull. 38:149-234.

Sette, O. E., and E. H. Ahlstrom. 1948. Estimations of abundance of eggs of the Pacific pilchard (*Sardinops caerulea*) off southern California during 1940 and 1941. J. Mar. Res. 7:511-542.

Shelbourne, J. E. 1964. The artificial propagation of marine fish.
Adv. Mar. Biol. 2:1-83.

Shelbourne, J. E. 1965. Rearing marine fish for commercial purposes.
Cal. Coop. Ocean. Fish. Invest. 10:53-63.

Shelbourne, J. E. 1974. Population effects on the survival, growth and
pigment of tank-reared plaice larvae. Pages 357-378 *in* F. R.
Harden Jones, ed. Sea Fish. Res. Elok Sci. London. 510 pp.

Simpson, A. C. 1956. The pelagic phase. Pages 207-250 *in* M. Graham,
ed. Sea fisheries, their investigation in the United Kingdom.
Arnold, London.

Simpson, A. C. 1951. The fecundity of the plaice. Fish. Invest. Lond.
17:1-28.

Simpson, A. C. 1959. The spawning of the plaice (*Pleuronectes
platessa*) in the North Sea. Fish. Invest. Lond. 2, 22(7). 111 pp.

Smith, L. L., Jr., and D. M. Oseid. 1974. Effect of hydrogen sulfide
on development and survival of eight freshwater fish species.
Pages 417-430 *in* J. H. S. Blaxter, ed. The early life history of
fish. Springer, Heidelberg.

Smith, P. E. 1973. The mortality and dispersal of sardine eggs and
larvae. Rapp. P.-V. Reun. ICES 164:282-292.

Smith, P. E., and S. L. Richardson. 1977. Standard techniques for
pelagic fish egg and larva surveys. FAO Fish. Tech. Pap.
No. 175. 100 pp.

Solemdal, P. 1967. The effect of salinity on buoyancy, size and
development of flounder eggs. Sarsia 29:431-442.

Solemdal, P. 1973. Transfer of Baltic flatfish to a marine environment
and the long term effects on reproduction. Oikos Suppl.
15:268-276.

Southward, A. J., and N. Demir. 1974. Seasonal changes in dimensions
and viability of the developing eggs of the cornish pilchard (*S.
pilchardus* Walbaum) off Plymouth. Pages 53-68 *in* J. H. S. Blaxter,
ed. The early life history of fish. Springer, Heidelberg.

Svardson, G. 1949. Natural selection and egg number in fish. Rep.
Inst. Freshw. Res. Drottningholm 29:115-122.

Talbot, J. W. 1977. The dispersal of plaice eggs and larvae in the
Southern Bight of the North Sea. J. Cons., ICES 37:221-248.

Tanaka, S. 1973. Stock assessment by means of ichthyoplankton surveys.
Pages 33-51 *in* G. Hempel, ed. Fish egg and larval surveys.
(Contributions to a manual.) FAO Fish. Tech. Pap. No. 122.

Tanaka, S. 1974. Significance of egg and larval surveys in the studies
of population dynamics of fish. Pages 151-157 *in* J. H. S. Blaxter,
ed. The early life history of fish. Springer, Heidelberg.

Taylor, F. H. C. 1971. Variation in hatching success in Pacific herring (*Clupea pallasii*) eggs with water depth, temperature, salinity, egg mass thickness. Rapp. P.-V. Réun. ICES 160:34-41.

Von Westernhagen, H. 1968. Versuche zur Erbrutung der Eier des Schellfisches (*Melanogrammus aeglefinus* L.) unter kombinierten Salzgehalt-und Temperaturvedingungen. Ber. dt. wiss. Kommn. Meeresforsch. 19:270-287.

Von Westernhagen, H. 1970. Erbrutung der Eier von Dorsh (*Gadus morhua*), Flounder (*Pleuronectes flesus*) und der Scholle (*Pleuronectes platessa*) unter kombinierten Temperaturund Salsgehaltsbedingungen. Helgolander Wiss. Meeresunters. 21:21-102.

Walford, L. A. 1938. Effect of current on distribution and survival of the eggs and larvae of the haddock (*Melanogrammus aeglefinus*). U.S. Bur. Fish., Fish. Bull. 49(29). 73 pp.

Wiborg, K. F. 1957. Factors influencing the size of the year-classes in the Arcto-Norwegian tribe of cod. Fiskeridir. Skr. Havundersøk. 2(8):1-24.